Abolitionists of the Northeast

Abolitionists of the Northeast

Black Leaders in the Antislavery Movement

GAIL BRACCIDIFERRO MACDONALD

Essex, Connecticut

Globe
Pequot

An imprint of The Globe Pequot Publishing Group, Inc.
64 South Main Street
Essex, CT 06426
www.globepequot.com

Copyright © 2026 by Gail Braccidiferro MacDonald

Front cover photos (from left): Prudence Crandall Museum, Connecticut Economic and Community Development; Library Company of Philadelphia/Annie Webb Papers Collection; Collection of the Massachusetts Historical Society; Creative Commons public domain/ Courtesy of National Portrait Gallery, Smithsonian Institution; Collection of the Newport Historical Society/Courtesy of the Rhode Island Black Heritage Society; Courtesy League of Women for Community Service. Back cover photos (from left): Courtesy National Abolition Hall of Fame and Museum; July 1895 edition of *The American Women's Journal*, Kansas Historical Society; Public domain, courtesy Jesse Nasta, PhD, Assistant Professor of the Practice, African American Studies, Wesleyan University.

All rights reserved. No part of this book may be reproduced in any form or by any electronic or mechanical means, including information storage and retrieval systems, without written permission from the publisher, except by a reviewer who may quote passages in a review.

British Library Cataloguing in Publication Information available

Library of Congress Cataloging-in-Publication Data available

ISBN 978-1-4930-9835-4 (cloth)
ISBN 978-1-4930-9194-2 (paper)
ISBN 978-1-4930-9195-9 (electronic)

Contents

Foreword and Acknowledgments   vii
Introduction   xi

CONNECTICUT   1
Jehiel C. Beman 7
Sarah Harris Fayerweather 13
David Ruggles 21
Pelleman Williams 27

MAINE   37
Charles Frederick Eastman 41
Robert Benjamin Lewis 46
Reuben Ruby 50
John Brown Russwurm 54

MASSACHUSETTS   63
Paul Cuffe 67
Charlotte Forten Grimké 72
Prince Hall 79
Lewis Hayden 84
William Cooper Nell 90
Sarah Parker Remond 95

NEW HAMPSHIRE   99
Julia Williams Garnet 103
Ona Marie Judge 108
Prince Whipple 114
Harriet Wilson 120

NEW YORK — 125
Henry Highland Garnet 129
Elizabeth Jennings Graham 134
Solomon Northup 139
James McCune Smith 146

RHODE ISLAND — 153
George T. Downing 159
George Fayerweather III 165
Isaac Rice 170

VERMONT — 175
Jeffrey Brace 179
Andrew Harris 185
Lemuel Haynes 190
Louden Langley 194

Bibliography — 201
About the Author — 220

Foreword and Acknowledgments

When I was a child during the 1960s and 1970s, most schools' American history lessons dealing with slavery focused only on the South and only on the years just preceding the Civil War. The lessons seemed to indicate that slavery was not of a very long duration and, in contrast to the shameful history of our Southern neighbors, we in the North were the "good guys," the ones who didn't enslave others and also led the fight for abolition.

As is so often the case with history, however, I much later came to understand that the story of slavery, racism, and abolition in the United States is more complex, nuanced, broader-based geographically, and longer in duration than those childhood history lessons would have us believe. Yet even as I grew to understand that slavery was as commonplace in Northern colonies and states as it was in Southern colonies and states, it was some aha moments of realization that led me down the path to what became this book.

While researching a previous book, for example, I learned about some of the complexities of abolitionists—those people I had for so long seen as the utmost in "good guys." Yes, they did work to end the institution of slavery in America, but not all of them were as "good" as I had envisioned. Many wanted to end the practice of owning other humans, but quite a number of them, maybe even a majority of them, did not take the logical next step: believing that Black Americans deserved the same basic rights and opportunities afforded to white Americans.

In addition, a sizable proportion of people who wanted an end to slavery in the antebellum period also believed deeply that Blacks and whites should never coexist with one another. Instead, they advocated that people of color be relocated en masse "back" to Africa, even though by the mid-nineteenth century, many Blacks in America had never seen or been to Africa.

Another distortion that was a takeaway from my childhood history lessons was that people of color were not involved in advocating for themselves during the often tumultuous and divisive, yet also hopeful, time period between the American Revolution and the Civil War. Indeed, except for a few people, such as Frederick Douglass and Harriet Tubman, about whom we were taught, Black Americans remained almost invisible in those lessons, wrongly portrayed as being silently passive about their freedom, their civil rights, and their future.

This was a major myth. People of color such as those profiled in this book, and so many more who are not profiled here, worked courageously and publicly to advance abolition and increase civil rights for members of their community. They did so in the face of continuous racism and the threat of violence. Many were harassed or even beaten savagely and targeted during riots that saw their houses, schools, and other community institutions attacked or destroyed by arson fires.

Although many Americans are now better informed about the extent and stretch of slavery in this country's history, the complexities of the antebellum period and Reconstruction continue to not be as widely appreciated as they should be. For example, the heroic feats of many nineteenth-century Black activists have been nearly forgotten or buried in the sands of time. At the same time, many Americans are unwilling to accept the sometimes grim realities of our history.

I hope this book serves to not only elucidate readers about the important work accomplished by so many Northern Black reformers, but also to deepen and expand the thinking about the length of time and the range of places where slavery was commonplace in the country. I hope, too, that it will help some understand the deep roots of racism in America and the tangled interconnectedness of Northern and Southern business, economic and social interests that perpetuated both slavery and racism. In addition, I hope these profiles show the humanity of these amazing people. They endured great isolation and fear and wanted only to be respected as human beings, live safely in their communities, and have the same educational, vocational, and financial opportunities as all other Americans.

This book has been numerous years in the making. The research and writing represents a long journey for me, one that would not have been possible without the help of many others. I'd like to now recognize and thank many of those who helped make this project possible.

Librarians are always a nonfiction writer's best friend, and so many assisted with this project. I'm especially grateful to those who oversee academic and special collections libraries, including the ones at Connecticut College and the University of Rhode Island.

In New Orleans, where I researched the family of Mary and Pelleman Williams, those at the *Amistad* Research Center located at Tulane University and at the Historic New Orleans Collection were vital in aiding my research. In addition, the great staff of Le Musée de FPC (Free People of Color Museum), and the Backstreet Cultural Museum expanded my knowledge of the complex history of race relations in that city.

Local historians also were invaluable to my research. I consulted with these fonts of knowledge in Vermont, Connecticut, Rhode Island, Maine, and Massachusetts. In Massachusetts, those at Salem State University, the David Ruggles Center for History and Education in Florence, and the Museum of African American History in Boston helped me to achieve a deeper understanding of the lives of many of the important Black activists featured in this book. In addition, those who helped resurrect essential aspects of Black history by forming Black Heritage Trails in various places, such as Boston; Portsmouth, New Hampshire; Portland, Maine; and New London, Connecticut, helped me to walk in the footsteps of abolitionists and activists.

I can't begin to thank and offer enough praise for all those unseen people who worked to ensure that so many of the stories of these important Black figures are now available online in digital format. Only those whose research once had to be conducted entirely by in-person trips to countless libraries and archives can appreciate the huge advancement it is to have so much information available via Internet searches. I was especially impressed that so much of the original writings of those featured in this book were available free online. Being able to read their exact words helped me see the humanity of these heroes.

Finally, I must acknowledge the love, unfailing support, and constant encouragement I was given by my husband. He urged me to push forward with this project, even when COVID-19 shutdowns seemed to put it permanently on hold, as well as when his cancer diagnosis diverted so much of our efforts to his health care. Although his death in 2022 meant I was unable to discuss or troubleshoot much of the research and writing with him as stories came together in their final form, I'm confident his spirit remains with me and urges me onward. Thank you, Bruce. I love you.

Introduction

Slavery existed in New England and New York for more than two hundred years. Slaves arrived with some of the earliest European settlers, and for decades, slavery was an accepted part of everyday life in the Northern colonies.

Owning a slave was a sign of one's status and wealth, and many clergymen, merchants, and businessmen owned slaves. These enslaved people kept house, cooked, did laundry, served meals, drove coaches, worked on farms, sailing vessels, or in their owners' businesses, and completed many other tasks at the behest of their owners. Their lives, the tasks they did, and their movements were under the complete control of their owners.

Northern slavery was no less dehumanizing or demeaning to the enslaved people than it was in the American South. Even as the Northeast became the stronghold of the nineteenth-century abolitionist movement, pro-slavery sentiment and racism remained prevalent in the region right up to and through the Civil War.

It was against these prevailing societal attitudes that a substantial number of Black people fought for an end to slavery and an expansion of their basic human rights: safe housing, good education, a legal say in governmental affairs, access to public spaces, voting rights, and basic respect. Often, this work was done at great risk to those who stood up for their rights. Activists were frequently attacked, threatened, and harassed.

Indigenous peoples were among the first to be subjugated. While we most often equate American slavery with enslaved Africans or those of African descent, many of the first slaves in New England were Indigenous people. The Pequot War in the 1630s and King Philip's War in the 1670s resulted in a large number of captive Natives who were kept enslaved locally, shipped to the West Indies sugar plantations, or sometimes traded for enslaved Africans.

INTRODUCTION

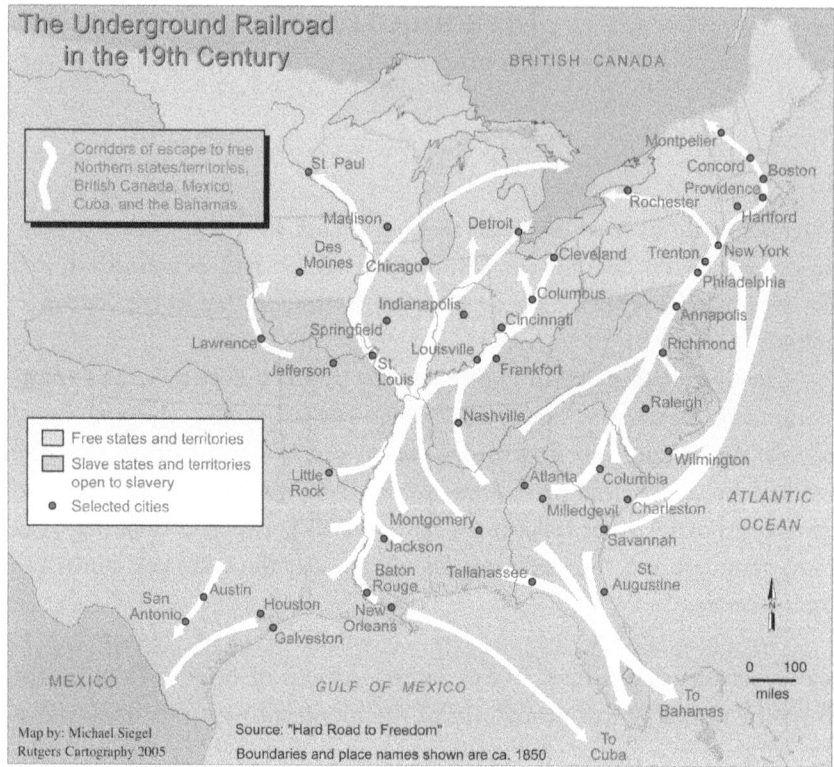

Underground Railroad routes, including those taking self-emancipating slaves through the Northeast. (Map by Michael Siegel, © Schomburg Center for Research in Black Culture, New York Public Library)

The first enslaved Africans arrived in Boston and Rhode Island in 1638. Dutch settlers brought enslaved Africans to what would become New York even earlier, in 1626. By the 1700s, there was a large number of slaves throughout the Northeast.

It wasn't until the Revolutionary War era that pushback against the institution of slavery became more common. People of color were not unaware of the revolutionary fervor surrounding them and seized upon these sentiments to advocate for their own freedom. The earliest outright abolition of slavery in the Northeast occurred in Vermont. Its 1777 constitution outlawed the practice, although it did not end racism or the prevailing societal attitudes that viewed people of color as subordinate to whites.

In most New England states and in New York, slavery did not end suddenly. With pro-slavery forces still strong in the Northeast, most states adopted laws resulting in a gradual elimination of the institution over a long period of time. Connecticut passed a gradual abolition law in 1784, for example, but did not completely abolish the practice of slavery until 1848. Rhode Island passed a gradual abolition law in 1784 as well, and completely abolished slavery in 1843. Massachusetts was an exception to this system, instead abolishing slavery outright just after the Revolution, in 1783. This law also applied to the territory that later became the state of Maine, but at that time was still part of Massachusetts.

Even after the practice was abolished in the Northeast, laws were flouted, with some enslaved people kept in the dark about their right to freedom. Ships carrying enslaved Africans continued to sail in and out of New York City, and slave catchers roamed throughout the region, snatching both self-emancipated slaves to return South and free Blacks, such as Solomon Northup of New York, who was duped into traveling with a pair of white hucksters who illegally sold him into slavery.

Life became even more dangerous for people of color after the Fugitive Slave Act of 1850 that punished those who aided self-emancipating slaves and allowed for the return of formerly enslaved people, even if they were residing in areas where slavery was outlawed.

Despite its duration, slavery in the North was definitively different from the system that developed in the South. Except for the large farms in what is now known as South County (or Washington County), Rhode Island, and a few places in eastern Connecticut, New England and New York did not have sprawling plantations of the type that developed in Southern states. While hundreds of slaves might toil on an individual Southern plantation, most Northern slave owners enslaved only a few individuals.

This did not mean, however, that Northern slavery was any less cruel, brutal, or dehumanizing. The slave narratives of Jeffrey Brace and Venture Smith, for example, chronicle extremely cruel treatment at the hands of New England slave owners. Harriet Wilson of New Hampshire wrote in her novel *Our Nig* about racist conditions and lived in abject poverty among Northern abolitionists.

Even when outright physical abuse was not present, the system of slavery, in both the North and the South, was built on dehumanization. Enslaved people's movements were controlled and limited. Most were not educated. They were clothed in whatever their owners handed them. Sometimes they were not provided shoes, despite the cold New England winters. Their food could be limited. They often slept on cold floors or in attic spaces that were freezing in winter and brutally hot in summer. Family separation was a looming threat.

By the 1700s, pushback against slavery had begun. In 1712, there was a very early slave revolt in New York City, but in general, it wasn't until more Blacks were being emancipated and general talk of freedom and liberty took hold in the American colonies during the Revolutionary War period that a wider skepticism of slavery began to spread. Many men of color fought in the Revolution—some for the British, because they were promised freedom in exchange for their service, and some for the Continentals. Some slave owners promised to manumit those who fought, but some reneged on this promise.

Just as the revolutionaries fought to end "taxation without representation," people of color advocated for voting privileges, access to education at all levels, equal access in public spaces and improved job opportunities.

Despite their courageous advocacy, history has mostly forgotten these important Black reformers. History lessons of abolition focus mainly on the white allies who fought beside Black people, but view the enslaved and free Black activists as voiceless and almost invisible. No doubt these white abolitionists were vital to the cause, but the view of a passive community of color is both skewed and inaccurate.

One of the most fearless Black abolitionists was David Ruggles, who was a founder of the New York Committee of Vigilance in 1835. Born in Connecticut, Ruggles spent most of his short life in New York City, where he regularly sought out and reported ships loaded with illegally held African captives bound for slavery, assisted self-emancipating slaves, and counseled many about the law. The vigilance committee aided more than one thousand freedom-seeking people of color, including Frederick Douglass, one of the few Black abolitionists whose legacy American history lessons do remember.

Ruggles, although considered a radical even by other abolitionists, was not alone in his battle. In 1779, for example, Prince Whipple of New Hampshire, along with a group of other Black men, petitioned the New Hampshire Council and House of Representatives to end slavery there. Paul Cuffe and a group of other Black men in Massachusetts in 1780 petitioned the state to be exempted from taxes on the basis of being unable to vote. Both pleas were ignored by lawmakers.

Some Blacks advocated for more drastic measures. In August 1843, for example, Henry Highland Garnet advocated for the enslaved to rise up and fight against their oppressors when he addressed the National Negro Convention in Buffalo, New York.

For people of color, the nineteenth century was both an intensely hopeful and uplifting period and a disheartening one. Advances in their cause were repeatedly met with setbacks and attacks. The promise of the abolitionist movement faced pressure from pro-slavery reformers, colonizationists who wanted all Blacks removed from the United States, as well as violence during events such as the New York City Draft Riots of 1863. Five days of arson, lynchings, beatings, and general mob violence in that city left more than one hundred Blacks dead and led many prominent members of the Black community to move out of Manhattan for good.

By the 1860s, the jubilation of emancipation and passage of the Thirteenth, Fourteenth, and Fifteenth Amendments—which opened voting rights, and led some Blacks to seek elective offices on local, state, and national levels—was met with the post-Reconstruction period with its rise of terrorists known as the Ku Klux Klan, along with repressive segregationist and Jim Crow laws.

It's difficult to imagine the depth of the hope that must have filled people such as Pelleman and Mary Williams and Charlotte Grimké as they headed to the South to teach newly freed slaves. It's equally as difficult to imagine the despair that must have enveloped them when more obstacles were erected against their community, including new laws enacted to thwart racial advancements.

People of color worked diligently for the expansion of rights gained during the nineteenth century. Unfortunately, their work was far from over when slavery ended.

In recent years, projects and new research are seeking to restore knowledge of slavery, its victims, and these brave activists who stood up and spoke out. Sculptures, monuments, heritage trails, and speaking programs are seeking to restore this important history to our consciousness. Projects such as the Witness Stones Project are restoring the names of those once enslaved in New England and marking the places where they lived and toiled.

Yet even as this happens, others seek to deny or once again erase this history. Each American has a role to play in ensuring this is prevented and that the tragedy of slavery is not forgotten, wherever it occurred, and that the important accomplishments of the great many people of color who fought back are always remembered.

Connecticut
A Public Deeply Divided on the Question of Slavery

In 1798 in New London, Connecticut, a small book was published recounting the experiences of an enslaved person. Venture Smith's story is among just a handful of slave narratives ever published. It tells the story of his capture from Africa, the brutal treatment and betrayals he suffered as an enslaved person in Connecticut, and his ultimate purchase of freedom for himself and his family.

The narrative of this remarkable enslaved person who persevered and fought back against injustice paints a picture of slavery in Connecticut that is every bit as brutal and dehumanizing as that practiced on any Southern plantation. One of Smith's owners, whose treatment of Smith was ruthless, was Thomas Stanton, a highly respected member of white society in Stonington.

Smith's story stands as stark evidence that slavery was a barbaric institution in the North as much as in the South. It also demonstrates its wide acceptance in colonial Connecticut. Joshua Hempstead, for example—the colonial-era New London diarist who recorded everyday life in the seacoast city for forty-seven years in the first half of the eighteenth century—wrote regularly about the work done by Adam Jackson. Hempstead enslaved Jackson for about thirty years.

The Hempsteads were hardly an anomaly in colonial Connecticut. As in other New England states, many wealthier white families owned slaves. These included Blacks whose backgrounds traced to Africa or the West Indies and Native Americans who were captured and enslaved following the Pequot War of 1637. In addition, the economy of Connecticut and its powerful institutions were inextricably intertwined with the slave trade. Not only did Connecticut mariners participate directly in the trade, but they also supplied food and other goods to West Indies plantations where African slaves' life expectancy was less than seven years. Heralded institutions of higher education such as Yale University also benefited from the slave trade, counting many slave-holding Southern elites among their alumni.

Much later, Connecticut's insurance businesses readily insured the human property on Southern plantations; its textile mills produced fabric used to clothe enslaved people; and the ivory trade in the Connecticut River Valley relied on enslaved labor in Africa.

At the time of the American Revolution, Connecticut was first among the New England colonies in terms of the number of slaves living within its borders. In the book *Complicity*, which details the state's long ties to slavery, the authors write that half of the state's ministers and most of its wealthy merchant class owned at least one slave by 1790. As of that year, there were 2,764 slaves living in the state. Also that year, a group of ministers beginning to lean into the anti-slavery cause formed the Connecticut Society for the Promotion of Freedom and the Relief of Persons Unlawfully Holden in Bondage.

Even as attitudes toward slavery changed and the institution was more often questioned and opposed, the state only gradually worked to abolish slavery. Connecticut blocked the importation of slaves in 1774, but it did not legislate against slavery in general. In 1784, it passed a Gradual Abolition Act. This act freed those born into slavery after March 1, 1784, when they turned twenty-five years old. The effect was that slavery was not fully abolished in Connecticut until 1848.

As Blacks and their white allies in the nineteenth century pressed for an end to slavery in the United States, along with increased civil rights for Blacks everywhere, events in Connecticut show a growing distaste for slavery alongside the strong clutch of racism on a large portion of society. The Connecticut Anti-Slavery Society was established in 1838, for example, but by then at least two high-profile series of events showing the strength of racism in the state had also played out.

In 1831, a group of abolitionists proposed what would have been the country's first college for Black men. They set their sights on New Haven as the place it would be established. The city was already the site of other noted educational institutions, including Yale. White citizens in the city turned out to overwhelmingly oppose the proposed college, however, voting 700 to 4 against it, and writing and speaking in derogatory terms about having such an influx of Black scholars in the city.

Just a year later, Prudence Crandall admitted a young Black woman to her well-respected female academy in rural Canterbury, located in eastern Connecticut. When parents of white students began pulling their daughters from the now-integrated school, Crandall temporarily closed it and reopened it as a school exclusively for young Black women. The resulting uproar in Canterbury led to a restrictive new so-called "Black Law" in Connecticut that prohibited the education of Black students within the state, unless local authorities approved. Crandall and her students were harassed and threatened, eventually leading Crandall to abandon her effort and leave Connecticut for good.

In contrast to the setbacks to the Black community caused by these two incidents, the story of the *Amistad* mutineers in Connecticut was a victory for those fighting slavery. On August 24, 1839, the schooner *Amistad* was found adrift off Long Island and taken to the customs house in New London. The fifty-three Africans aboard had been illegally abducted by Portuguese slave hunters. They were being transported to a plantation in the West Indies when they took control of the ship and ordered it to be sailed back to Africa. Instead, the vessel ended up off the Connecticut coastline.

Abolitionists supported the mutineers in their quest to be returned to Africa. Many of the Africans were housed and supported by abolitionists in Farmington as the case made its way through the courts. Ultimately, the US Supreme Court decided in their favor, ruling that the Africans had the right to resist illegal slavery. While some of the mutineers had died at sea or while awaiting trial, thirty-five eventually returned to Africa.

Noted white Connecticut abolitionists also aided Blacks in their fight. Most notably, Harriet Beecher Stowe, who was born in Litchfield and later lived in Hartford, wrote a book long noted as pivotal in educating the public about the evils of slavery. *Uncle Tom's Cabin* was released in 1852 and sold 300,000 copies during its first year of publication.

Today, Connecticut recognizes and celebrates the important contributions of people of color throughout its history in numerous ways. A program called Discovering *Amistad*, for example, uses a reproduction of the original schooner that carried the African mutineers to educate children and adults about the nineteenth-century events. An exhibition focused on the *Amistad* case is on view at the New London Custom House Maritime Museum.

Other programs include the Witness Stones Project that has installed markers commemorating enslaved people who lived and worked in Guilford, West Hartford, Madison, Norfolk, New Haven, Cos Cob, Old Lyme, Killingly, Dayville, Suffield, Danbury, Hartford, Hebron, Norwich, Essex, Ridgefield, Woodstock, Stonington, Brooklyn, Bethlehem, Hamden, Old Saybrook, Plainfield, Wallingford, Durham, Manchester, New London, Mansfield, Wilton, Branford, Farmington, Southington, Riverton, and Brooklyn.

In addition, the Connecticut Freedom Trail and New London Black Heritage Trail were developed to recognize significant Black residents from the past and celebrate their accomplishments. And in New Haven, a monument honoring the state's Black Civil War soldiers was installed in 2008. Some nine hundred soldiers fought with the Connecticut 29th Colored Regiment.

The Prudence Crandall Museum. Crandall opened her school for Black girls here in 1833. (Author's Collection)

Jehiel C. Beman

Minister, Abolitionist, and Temperance Leader

Jehiel C. Beman. (Public Domain / Courtesy Jesse Nasta, PhD, Assistant Professor of the Practice, African American Studies, Wesleyan University)

Two of the original Beman Triangle houses in Middletown, Connecticut. (Author's Collection)

Jehiel C. Beman

On September 7, 1854, Jehiel C. Beman wrote from Middletown, Connecticut, to Frederick Douglass, one of the most noted Black abolitionists in the country: "I would inform you that we have had a recent arrival from the land of chains and whips, where the image of the Divine Being is bought and sold. The Underground Railroad, by the way, is in good repair, and our office is open for business in our line, at all hours, either day or night, and our cars run on the Trail."

In 1830, Beman became the first regular pastor at Connecticut's first Black church—Middletown's Cross Street AME Zion Church. He was a leader of the Black community in Middletown and traveled extensively throughout the state, preaching about abolitionism and Black civil rights. He was an abolitionist, an advocate for equality of educational opportunities for members of his community, a leader of the temperance movement, and a proponent of voting rights for Blacks. His writings were published in abolitionist newspapers.

Beman and his family came to Middletown at a time when the city's Black community was growing and the abolition movement was gaining strength and adherents. He and several of his family members worked tirelessly to improve the lives of Black people, and they succeeded in some respects. While so many gains seemed destined to face pushback from racist opponents, the Bemans dedicated their lives to the pursuit of racial civil rights nonetheless.

He closed the letter to Douglass about his involvement in the Underground Railroad in this manner: "And now, dear Sir, if you will have the goodness to recommend our road to the travelling public, you will oblige the Association. Yours, for the Oppressed, JCB."

The Bemans' dedication to abolition and Black rights began with Jehiel's father. In fact, the Beman name began with Jehiel's father.

Cesar Beman was among some three hundred Black Connecticut Revolutionary War soldiers. He likely was freed because of that service. When he was freed, he took a new last name. His son Jehiel noted when corresponding with a person writing about the history of Blacks in New England, "My father always abhorred slavery and he wanted to 'be a man.' So, when he was freed, he took the name Beman. Be a man." The anecdote was included in a 2020 WSHU public radio broadcast focused on the Bemans.

In 1844, on a trip to Washington, DC, Jehiel Beman recalled his parents' enslavement as he observed enslaved people working in the fields through the train window. Some of his observations were published in an abolitionist newspaper: "But in the fields, to see my sisters toiling, pitchfork and rake in hand, under the scorching rays of the sun, with no covering on the head, and but little on the body—as this was the first scene of the kind I ever saw, my feelings were such as I cannot describe."

Beman grew up in Colchester, located in eastern Connecticut. He attended the African schoolhouse there, and later worked as both a minister and a shoemaker. He married and had seven children, although his first wife died shortly after they moved to Middletown. He continued working as a shoemaker while also leading his congregation in Middletown.

Middletown, located on the Connecticut River, was an important port during colonial times, and the maritime trades during that time period included involvement in the African slave trade. A UNESCO Slave Route Project plaque was unveiled on the Middletown waterfront in 2019. It notes that in 1738, the ship *Martha & Jane* arrived in Middletown from Africa with 125 enslaved Africans aboard. Another 23 died on the journey. In 1761, the ship *Speedwell* also arrived with enslaved Africans; 74 survived the voyage, and 21 died in the Middle Passage.

On the eve of the American Revolution, more than two hundred Blacks, most of whom were enslaved, lived in Middletown. By the 1820s, the now mostly free Black population remained at about the same level, but westward migration by whites was creating job opportunities for Blacks. As some Blacks moved into cities, relatively significant Black communities were established in Middletown, Norwich, New London, and other localities.

When the Bemans moved to Middletown, they soon became leaders of the Black community there. Jehiel Beman was a founding member of the Middletown Anti-Slavery Society in 1834. His second wife Nancy and his daughter-in-law Clarissa cofounded one of the first female anti-slavery societies, called the Colored Females' Anti-Slavery Society of Middletown. The church Jehiel led hosted abolitionist speakers who included Douglass and William Lloyd Garrison. As evidenced in Beman's letter to Douglass, as a stop on the Underground Railroad, the church also sheltered enslaved people who were seeking their freedom.

As the Bemans and other members of Middletown's Black community struggled to promote the cause of abolition, they also faced those who pushed back violently against their efforts. In 1835, for example, an anti-abolitionist riot broke out on Cross Street. Beman himself was sometimes subjected to physical violence.

Besides their abolitionist work, the Bemans believed deeply in promoting more educational opportunities for Blacks. In 1832, Beman wrote, "Since it is said that knowledge is power, does it not become us to use that power in governing ourselves?"

When a college for Black men was proposed in New Haven in 1831, Beman diligently raised funds for the institution. Advocates of the college proposed that $10,000 should be raised from Black donors and an equal amount from white donors. The college's planners chose New Haven, in part because they believed residents there would support it, and at first the plan seemed to gain public acceptance, judging by some contemporary newspaper accounts.

As abolitionism spread, so, too, did anti-Black sentiment, fueled by incidents such as Nat Turner's Rebellion, an 1831 Virginia slave uprising in which fifty-five whites were killed, spreading fear among the white population. Following the incident, more than thirty-six enslaved people were killed in retaliation, without trial, and another thirty were condemned to death after trial.

Pro-slavery elites in New Haven were eager to kill the college proposal. At a town meeting, seven hundred residents opposed the college, and just four supported it. The opposition was led by David Daggett, a judge and one of the founders of the Yale Law School. The resolution drafted by opponents read, in part: "The propagation of sentiments favorable to the immediate emancipation of slaves in disregard of the civil institutions of the States in which they belong, and as auxiliary thereto the contemporaneous founding of Colleges for educating colored people, is unwarrantable and dangerous interference with the internal concerns of other States, and ought to be discouraged."

Despite these setbacks, Beman's work on behalf of the Black community continued. In 1833, he formed the Home Temperance Society out of his belief that alcohol was a scourge in his community. Three years later, he was instrumental in forming the Connecticut State Temperance Society of Colored People. A year after its founding, it counted some 350 members.

Beginning in the late 1830s, Beman moved away from and then back to Middletown several times. He led the congregation at Zion's Church in Boston beginning in 1838.

The family's contributions to Middletown continued, including one of their most significant actions: working to increase homeownership among Black families. Property ownership was viewed as an important step toward full enfranchisement of Blacks, as important as gaining equitable educational opportunities and voting rights. The ability for Blacks to buy property was severely restricted, however, due to the racial prejudice that made it difficult for them to secure loans or find property owners willing to sell to them.

In 1846, Leverett Beman, one of Jehiel's sons, bought a three-and-a-half-acre parcel of land bounded by Cross and Vine streets and Knowles Avenue, which at that point was known as Swamp Street. Leverett subdivided the parcel into eleven house lots. Five of them were already owned by Black families. He sold the rest to other Black families, creating a rarity, and probably a first for Connecticut—a completely Black-owned neighborhood.

While the Beman Triangle, so named because of its shape, was a remarkable achievement, the land also was substandard, swampy and prone to flooding—likely one of the reasons it could be acquired by Blacks. Years later, when Black families moved away from the neighborhood, it became home to immigrant communities. The area, now owned primarily by Wesleyan University, is a historic district. Half of the original Black-owned homes remain.

Jehiel Beman died in 1858 in New York City, but was buried in his beloved Middletown, where he had dedicated his life to improving the lives of the Black community.

Sarah Harris Fayerweather
Quest for an Education Sparks a Racial Crisis

Sarah Harris Fayerweather, late in life. (Prudence Crandall Museum, Connecticut Economic and Community Development)

On July 26, 1871, Prudence Crandall wrote a letter from her home in Kansas to Sarah Harris Fayerweather in Rhode Island: "You do not know how I value every word you write. I have no friend on earth I would more rejoice to see than yourself." Later in the same letter, she referred to her very elderly and ill mother: "If I could leave my mother, I would visit you if permitted. I do want you to come out here very much indeed."

Crandall was sixty-seven years old at the time. Fayerweather was fifty-nine. The two women had been friends for some forty years at that point, and together experienced some harrowing occurrences in Connecticut.

Sarah Harris Fayerweather did finally visit her longtime friend, but it would be another seven years before she took the grueling trip. Even in her final years, she did not shy away from facing challenges head-on.

In April 1878, she boarded a steam-powered train at Kingston Station in Rhode Island, switching train lines numerous times until she reached Independence, Kansas. Then, she took a stagecoach another thirty-five miles to the tiny prairie town of Elk Falls, and, finally, hired a wagon to take her about a mile to the isolated, barebones farmhouse where Crandall lived. The trip would have been exhausting for anyone, but for a Black woman traveling alone, the challenges presented by racism would have made it even more potentially harrowing.

When Fayerweather finally arrived at Crandall's home, she was greeted by a young niece of Crandall's who said she found Fayerweather a fine-looking woman with wavy white hair. Crandall and Fayerweather visited for two weeks before Fayerweather returned to Rhode Island. The timing of the trip was fortuitous, as within about seven months, Fayerweather would be dead.

Donald Williams of Connecticut, one of Crandall's biographers, said Crandall was viewed as an oddity in the rural southeastern corner of Kansas where she spent her final years. She had become entrenched in spiritualism and had aspirations of starting a school for Blacks on the site of her home. Still, given her fight over racial issues in Connecticut, which in 1995 would earn her the title of the state's heroine, it seems fitting she ended up in a state where race played a big part in its settlement and admission to the Union as a free state. Kansas also was the location of a western branch of the Underground Railroad that aided escaped slaves traveling to freedom, the site of a historically Black college established in 1865, and a destination for many newly freed Blacks following the Civil War.

Long before Crandall settled in Kansas, she and Sarah Harris were responsible for touching off a crisis of sorts in Connecticut in which both extreme courage and shameful racism played roles. While Crandall's heroism was ultimately recognized in Connecticut, Sarah Harris's lifelong activism is less known and appreciated.

Sarah Harris grew up in Norwich, Connecticut, one of twelve children of William Monteflora Harris and Sally Prentice. The family of color had roots in Africa, the West Indies—likely Haiti, where the world's first Black republic was established in 1804—and among local Native tribes. Sarah spent her childhood in the Jail Hill neighborhood of Norwich, an area perched high atop steep hillsides overlooking the small eastern Connecticut city's harbor, near the head of the Thames River. Probably due to its challenging topography, it was not a desirable neighborhood for wealthier residents, but was home to a thriving, largely Black, and activist community.

William Harris became an agent for the radical abolitionist newspaper *The Liberator*, and several family members served as representatives to Colored Men's Conventions in which issues such as the abolition of slavery, voting rights, and educational equality were discussed. They belonged to a church in which abolition was a frequent topic, and they regularly attended meetings where participants advocated for the end of slavery and advancing equal rights for Blacks. Their church, the Second Congregational Church of Norwich, also operated an integrated church school, and espoused the rare contemporary sentiment of racial equality.

Despite being surrounded by like-minded neighbors, William Harris's desire to own land must have been stronger than his need for a close social circle. In 1832, via a deed filed in his wife's name, he bought for $900 a farm in the rural community of Canterbury, Connecticut, about fifteen miles northeast of Norwich. He moved his family there.

It was here that Sarah Harris and Prudence Crandall made history in the sleepy, tiny town. In the fall of 1832, Sarah asked to be admitted to the private girls' school Crandall ran from her home, just off the town green. Crandall didn't immediately accept Harris as a student. Although she had converted to the Baptist denomination in 1831, it's likely that her earlier Quaker upbringing led her to the conclusion it was the right thing to do. Quakers were the first religious organization to condemn slavery, and as early as the mid-eighteenth century, they were actively working to abolish the institution. In addition, Crandall had become acquainted with and influenced by the writings in the abolitionist newspaper *The Liberator*, published by William Lloyd Garrison.

Harris, who had received basic education as a child in local schools, requested admittance to Crandall's academy so she could learn enough to become a teacher herself. She said she hoped to teach children of color, but indicated to Crandall, "If you think it will be the means of injuring you, I will not insist on the favor."

Crandall admitted Sarah to her academy. Although she was already twenty years old at the time of her admission, Sarah was generally accepted by the white students. Many of their families were aghast, however, and promptly withdrew their daughters from Crandall's school. Local residents also began to agitate against it. Crandall, facing tough financial times because of the dwindling number of students, consulted with local abolitionists, including Garrison, the leading abolitionist in New England. She ultimately decided to dismiss all of her white students and reopen the school exclusively to girls of color.

A campaign of harassment and threats by her neighbors ensued. Thugs threw rocks through the schoolhouse windows and tainted the well with manure. They hung the body of a mangled cat at the property. Some merchants refused to sell goods to the school.

Some of the most virulent criticism was waged by Andrew Judson, one of Crandall's neighbors. Judson was a wealthy and well-respected politician, attorney, and judge. He was also an avowed racist. In an April 1833 letter, Prudence Crandall wrote, "The thought of such opposition as has been raised in the minds of the people of Canterbury and the adjoining towns never once entered into my mind while contemplating the change I am now endeavoring to effect in my school."

Judson, like many others at the time, believed in what was called "colonization." Under such a plan, all Black residents of the United States would be resettled in Africa. Many colonizationists believed Blacks were inferior, and that Blacks and whites should not live side by side.

An article first printed in the *Norwich Republican* and reprinted on April 6, 1833, in Garrison's *The Liberator*, well illustrates the local attitude against Crandall. After denouncing abolitionists as supporting and advocating for the school, the article goes on to say:

> *And what do they propose to do by means of this institution? Why, to break down the barriers which God has placed between blacks and whites—to manufacture "young ladies of color," and to foist upon the community a new species of gentility, in the shape of sable belles. They propose, by softening down the rough features of the African mind in these wenches, to cook up a palatable morsel for our white bachelors. After this precious concoction is completed, they are then to be taken by the hand, introduced into the best society, and made to aspire to the first matrimonial connections in the country. In a word, they hope to force the two races to amalgamate!*

This threat of interracial marriage was used again and again to foment racist fear and hatred among whites during the antebellum period, and beyond.

Seeking to eliminate the school, Judson succeeded in getting the state legislature to pass a notorious Black Law that banned educating Black students from out of state without the approval of local authorities. Although Crandall entered into an extended legal battle challenging the law, the harassment against her school continued, and, fearing for her students' safety, she decided in the fall of 1834 to close it permanently.

Sarah Harris, meanwhile, exchanged her dream of becoming a teacher to instead marry and raise a family. When she was twenty-one years old, in 1833, she married George Fayerweather, age thirty-one, in a double ceremony with her brother Charles and his bride Anna Mariah

Davis. The couples married at the Westminster Congregational Church in Canterbury.

The September 9, 1834, mob attack on Crandall's school that ultimately led to Crandall's decision to close it occurred on the same day Sarah and George celebrated the birth of their first child, who they named Prudence Crandall Fayerweather. They would go on to have as many as eight more children, although the exact number is somewhat uncertain, with some sources indicating they had just four children.

The Fayerweathers moved to New London, Connecticut, about fifteen miles south of Norwich and located at the mouth of the Thames River. George, whose father and grandfather were both blacksmiths, also took up that trade, and owned his New London shop. Blacksmithing was a popular profession among the Black community. It was essential in that era, not only because of the heavy reliance on horses, but also because the whaling industry relied on tools fabricated in blacksmith shops.

Along with her increasing domestic duties, Sarah Harris Fayerweather continued to be active in the anti-slavery movement. She frequently attended abolitionist conventions and became friends with Garrison, sending a fruitcake to his family each Christmas.

The Fayerweathers also hosted noted abolitionists at their home. When the family moved from New London to Kingston, Rhode Island, where George had been raised, they not only hosted Garrison, but also the preeminent abolitionist Frederick Douglass. It has also been said that they served as conductors on the Underground Railroad.

When Garrison was invited to attend a ceremony at Fort Sumter to commemorate the end of the Civil War, Fayerweather wrote to him: "I praise the name of the Lord that he has prolonged your precious life to see this day. My joy is full when I think of your being at Charleston, South Carolina, having those very slaves for whom you have toiled a persecuted lifetime bowing down at your garment."

The Fayerweathers, and others who fought hard and long to end slavery and advance the condition of people of color in the country, rejoiced at Abraham Lincoln's 1863 Emancipation Proclamation. They celebrated the passage of the Thirteenth, Fourteenth, and Fifteenth

Amendments and the programs of Reconstruction in the South. Even so, they would come to understand that an end to slavery did not mean the end of harassment and discrimination for Blacks.

Fayerweather's dedication to the causes of equal rights and justice for all Americans never wavered, however, and is evident in the correspondence that for decades she kept up with Prudence Crandall, whose life proved more tumultuous and uncertain than Fayerweather's.

Near the tail end of her struggles in Canterbury, Crandall married Calvin Philleo, a fiery minister. A widower with two children, Philleo was mentally unstable. The couple moved to Illinois, but frequently lived apart from one another.

Calvin Philleo's daughter by his first marriage met Sarah Harris Fayerweather in 1863, at a meeting of the Massachusetts Anti-Slavery Society in Boston. She wrote, "I invited her to come and pass the afternoon with me, and I wish you could have been here to hear her talk of the days of Mother's [Crandall's] persecution, and also to hear many things about Mother, for whom she entertains the warmest love and gratitude. . . . I do not know when I have enjoyed an afternoon better than in this woman's society. She is very intelligent and lady-like, well informed in every movement relative to the removal of slavery, and converses very well."

Fayerweather and Philleo continued to correspond regularly, sharing news of each other's families, including the death of George Fayerweather in 1869, and frequently discussing developments in the quest for racial equality for which they both worked.

"I thank God that Garrison has lived to see the shackles fall from the slave," Philleo wrote in 1863. "And oh, the glorious future that will result of the labors of God's noble ones both colored and white."

When Crandall sold her Illinois farm, she moved to Kansas. The frequent letters between her and her old friend from Connecticut culminated in the two-week visit by Fayerweather to Kansas in 1878.

While Philleo lived until 1890, just a short time after her friend returned to Rhode Island, Fayerweather was plagued by a swelling in her neck that caused her to lose her ability to speak. Many years earlier, in a letter to Sarah, her mother cautioned her to not have an operation for a goiter on her neck, which is a swelling of the thyroid gland.

Sarah Harris Fayerweather died on November 16, 1878, and is buried next to her husband in the family plot in the Old Fernwood Cemetery near Kingston, Rhode Island. Her accomplishments were recognized by the nearby University of Rhode Island, which in 1979 named a dormitory building in her honor.

David Ruggles
Bold and Courageous Anti-Slavery Crusader

In May 1835, a pamphlet published in New York City connected the institution of slavery with violations of the Seventh Commandment, which exhorts against adultery. Titled "The Abrogation of the Seventh Commandment by the American Churches," the twenty-two-page pamphlet details the proliferation of sexual intercourse between slaveholders and the females they held in slavery and the hypocrisy of so-called Christians who turned a blind eye to these acts. The pamphlet further delves into the fact that slavery, by prohibiting marriage between enslaved men and women, also gave license to violations of the commandment. Finally, the pamphlet calls upon women to petition against such actions and boycott churches that condoned or ignored them.

"It may not be accurately comprehended by you, that in addition to all the other most odious and criminal attributes of American slaveholding, a licentiousness of intercourse between the sexes, constant, incestuous, and universal, exists; the aggravated corruptions of which, no pen can describe, and no unpolluted imagination conceive," the pamphleteer wrote. And later: "The temptation from pecuniary advantage with all rapidity to multiply slaves, is equivalent to a bribe for impurity."

The pamphlet's author was David Ruggles, a bold, uncompromising, straight-talking, courageous, and unrelenting activist who would stop at nothing in his fight against slavery and the promotion of equal rights and opportunities for people of color. The pamphlet, with its direct language and taboo subject matter, especially by mid-nineteenth-century standards, is only one example of the many daring anti-slavery battles he fought during his short lifetime.

Ruggles repeatedly and fearlessly stood up to bigots and racists who harmed him physically as he strove to provide assistance and opportunities to those who fled slavery in the South. He promoted abolitionist newspapers; wrote and printed his own abolitionist magazine; operated a reading room and lending library for Black residents at a time when they were not allowed in libraries used by whites; and supported the free produce movement that boycotted all goods produced by slave labor. Ruggles also frequently sought out enslaved people being held illegally in New York City and counseled them on their legal rights. The Museum of the City of New York extols his important work in an exhibit called *Abolishing Slavery*: "In fewer than 15 years in the city, he had helped to radicalize the Black antislavery movement and to build an underground network that would, over the next decades, bring hundreds of enslaved people to freedom."

Ruggles likely started forming his anti-slavery opinions as a boy growing up in Norwich, Connecticut. He was born in 1810 in Lyme, the eldest of seven children, to parents who were both respected tradespeople. A free Black family, his mother was a caterer and his father, a blacksmith. When Ruggles was very young, the family moved to the Bean Hill neighborhood, located in the northern end of the small city of Norwich. His early education was at religious charity schools. His childhood was as peaceful as was possible for Black families at the time. There was a sizable population of free Blacks in Norwich, and the city became a regional focal point for abolitionist thought, speeches, and activities.

While numerous articles about Ruggles point out that he was highly intelligent, a prodigy of sorts, he would have been denied a higher education at the likes of Yale College because of the color of his skin. Yale would not admit a Black student until 1870.

Like many other young Blacks of his era, Ruggles decided on a life as a mariner when he was just fifteen years old. But by age seventeen, he had settled back on land—Lower Manhattan, in New York City. He opened a grocery store on Cortlandt Street in 1828, likely selling liquor along with food, as was common at the time. He changed that practice, however, after seeing the dysfunction and destruction alcohol consumption could cause. Ruggles unabashedly hired self-emancipated Black people to work at the store, which was torched twice by arsonists.

Ruggles soon learned that one of his greatest weapons in the anti-slavery fight was the written word. He is credited with being the country's first Black journalist, printing his own incendiary pamphlets, such as the one pointing out the proliferation of adultery in the institution of slavery, regularly writing editorials and letters to many newspapers, as well as also publishing his own anti-slavery publication, *The Mirror of Liberty*.

None of these activities was benign. In a city where pro-slavery sentiment and racism was strong, Ruggles regularly faced danger. Anti-abolitionist riots tore through the city in the summer of 1834, and slave catchers regularly snatched both free and formerly enslaved Blacks off the streets and shipped them south into servitude.

David Ruggles as depicted in a political cartoon of the era. (Courtesy of www.periodyssey.com)

He was undeterred. In November 1835, Ruggles was at the forefront of establishing the New York Committee of Vigilance, a multiracial group that sought to defend Blacks against white predators, including the police and corrupt city officials. Tom Goldscheider, education coordinator for the David Ruggles Center for History and Education in Northampton, Massachusetts, called this committee the forerunner of the NAACP. A plaque erected at the site of the committee's headquarters by the New York Landmarks Preservation Foundation notes that the committee aided more than one thousand freedom-seeking men, women, and children.

Ruggles took a decidedly reformer approach to the work and was considered an extreme radical, even by others who shared his views about slavery. Not content to simply sponsor anti-slavery speakers or hold meetings, he regularly prowled the New York City docks where ships carrying humans bound for slavery could be found, despite the 1808 US ban on the international slave trade.

In December 1836, for example, Ruggles learned that a Portuguese brig called the *Brilliante* was in port, carrying enslaved men. The story of the *Brilliante* is told in detail in an article written by Isaac Kolding, published on the Commonplace history website. Ruggles's discovery of the ship resulted in weeks of frustrating and largely fruitless machinations between Ruggles, the New York district attorney, and local law enforcement officials. The officials delayed action or ignored the situation while Ruggles wrote about the inaction in an effort to publicly embarrass them.

The enslaved men were moved into debtors' prison at one point, then returned to the ship. On Christmas Eve, a mob of Black men, which reportedly did not include Ruggles, stormed the ship and rescued two of the men. In retaliation, Ruggles was awoken on December 28 by pounding on his door. He escaped the three men carrying knives and pistols who forced open his door, and later sought to have them arrested. Instead of the justice he sought, however, Ruggles himself was arrested. While he was held only for a short time, the action was an ultimate insult in retribution for his attempts to see that federal law against the slave trade was upheld.

Ruggles also is considered among the first so-called conductors on the Underground Railroad. In September 1838, Ruggles encountered a man named Frederick Washington Bailey, who escaped slavery in Maryland and was struggling to survive in New York City. Bailey later wrote about the experience: "I had been in New York but a few days, when Mr. Ruggles sought me out, and very kindly took me to his boarding-house at the corner of Church and Lispenard streets." He also wrote, "Mr. Ruggles was the first officer on the Underground Railroad with whom I met after reaching the north. . . . He was a wholesouled man, fully imbued with a love of his afflicted and hunted people."

Ruggles housed Bailey and helped him reunite with his fiancée. The couple was married in Ruggles's house. A short time later, Ruggles sent them on to New Bedford, Massachusetts, with a letter of recommendation and five dollars. Bailey would change his name and become one of the best-known abolitionists and anti-slavery orators in the United States—Frederick Douglass.

The defiant, unapologetic means Ruggles employed in his work took a toll on both his health and his personal relationships. He frequently was injured in skirmishes with white racists, and a disagreement between him and one of his mentors, Samuel Cornish, led to an audit of the Vigilance Committee that resulted in Ruggles being ousted as secretary. The committee's financial shortfalls that were discovered likely stemmed from Ruggles's practice of giving five dollars to each of the self-emancipated he helped along on the Underground Railroad.

Before he had even reached the age of thirty, Ruggles was suffering from severe bowel disorders and was nearly blind. Lydia Maria Child, editor of the *National Anti-Slavery Standard*, encouraged Ruggles to get out of the hotbed of danger that was New York City and come live at an abolitionist utopian community in the small village of Florence in Northampton, Massachusetts. Called the Northampton Association of Education and Industry, the racially integrated community operated a silk mill as a worker-owned cooperative, grew sugar beets, and strove to live without goods produced by slave labor. They supported an immediate end to slavery and full rights of citizenship for all free Blacks. The community attracted some who had fled Southern slavery, including Sojourner Truth.

It was in Northampton that Ruggles learned of a then-trendy health practice called the water cure. He took the cure himself, and after experiencing some improvement from his own health travails, became a water cure practitioner himself.

Ruggles's ailments soon returned, however. As his health deteriorated, his mother and one of his sisters traveled from Connecticut in an effort to help him. Their efforts were in vain, and he died at the age of thirty-nine on December 16, 1849. Ruggles's body was returned to his home city of Norwich, where he was buried near his childhood neighborhood of Bean Hill, now a historic district.

Today, there is little evidence in the serene village of Florence of the utopian community that was considered profoundly radical by the general populace at the time. The small clapboard building that houses the David Ruggles Center for History and Education sits across a busy street from the site of the utopian community's former silk mill. A building where individuals took the water cure still stands, along with some of the houses members of the community lived in, including those once occupied by Ruggles and Sojourner Truth. The center's small museum, along with frequently sponsored walking tours and an African American Heritage Trail, help keep alive the monumental history that took place there in the 1840s.

Pelleman Williams
Dedicated to Educating Children of Color

On September 7, 1871, the *Weekly Louisianian* published an announcement: Professor P. M. Williams was the newly appointed keeper of the Boys House of Refuge in the city of New Orleans. The institution located outside the downtown area was built in 1849 and charged with housing, educating, and caring for juvenile offenders.

While some of these offenders' only crimes likely were being born poor and Black, the job of overseeing the institution no doubt was a challenging one, and the societal attitude toward the children is evident in the announcement. "Mr. Williams has had a protracted and varied experience in dealing with the wilfulness and waywardness of youth, and with the advantages of a persuasive disposition, we have no doubt his appointment will be found a wise one," the article read.

P. M. Williams, whose full first name was Pelleman (or Pelluman, depending on the document bearing the name), was already in his mid-fifties by the time he took over the leadership of the Boys House of Refuge, but his dedication to educating children of color from all sorts of backgrounds remained unwavering. He had decades of experience as an educator by the time of this appointment, sometimes working in extremely challenging conditions. He would continue working as a teacher for children of color until the day he died, in 1882.

Education has long been accepted as essential to socioeconomic and professional advancement, so it's no surprise it was a cornerstone during the nineteenth-century struggle to end slavery and elevate the status of people of color in the United States. In fact, this was the case even earlier. In the preface to the autobiography of Venture Smith—a man captured in West Africa as a child, enslaved in colonial Connecticut, and who eventually purchased freedom for himself and his family (along with real estate) before he died in 1805—the anonymous writer notes that Smith might have achieved even more in his already amazing lifetime with more advanced education. By the antebellum period, the great abolitionist leader and former slave Frederick Douglass also frequently linked the importance of literacy and education to freedom and elevation of status for Blacks.

Slaveholders also understood that education could dramatically impact the lives of their human property. They saw the education of Blacks as a dangerous threat, and did everything in their power to prevent Blacks from becoming literate or being allowed to think freely. In Virginia, Nat Turner led a successful slave revolt in 1831 that left some fifty-five white residents dead, and slaveholders' fears mounted further. In response to the rebellion, every slave-holding state except Maryland, Kentucky, and Tennessee passed laws making it illegal to teach slaves to read and write, according to a paper titled "Literacy as Freedom" by the Smithsonian American Art Museum. The paper also notes an article published in *Harper's Weekly* at about the time of the slave uprising, which indicated "the alphabet is an abolitionist. If you would keep a people enslaved, refuse to teach them to read."

It was in this atmosphere that the Williams family, and others who worked tirelessly for more racial equity in the nineteenth century, not only talked about the importance of education, but worked to provide it to people of color. Pelleman Williams and his wife strove throughout much of the nineteenth century for more educational opportunities for themselves and others of color from all socioeconomic strata. They never backed down, even in the face of the most vile racism, harassment, acts of vandalism and arson, and threats on their lives. Williams and his family dedicated their lives to this pursuit. And although they witnessed some great progress in their lifetimes, the 1800s ultimately ended with disappointing setbacks for Blacks, and with many more battles to be fought far into the future.

Pelleman Williams was a widely known and well-respected member of the free Black community in the North. Born in West Springfield, Massachusetts, in 1815, Williams grew up in a community where antislavery sentiment was common, where escaped slaves found refuge, and where a Black man named Peter Swinck had become one of the first of his race to own property in the second half of the 1600s, according to Joseph Carvalho III's book *Uncovering the Stories of Black Families in Springfield and Hampden County, Massachusetts: 1650–1865*.

Williams likely found this atmosphere empowering, and he went on to break racial barriers himself. He was, for example, among the first Black students to enroll at both Amherst and Dartmouth colleges. He was a member of the Dartmouth Class of 1845, but college archives list him as not graduating. Instead, he was working as a teacher by the time he might have been graduating with his classmates, marrying Mary Harris in April of that year.

Williams had met Mary while living in Connecticut. She was a member of a well-respected Black family who lived for years in Norwich before moving to the rural farming community of Canterbury. Mary's father was an agent for William Lloyd Garrison's abolitionist newspaper *The Liberator*, and the family was at the epicenter of one of the country's fiercest nineteenth-century fights over the right to a quality education for children of color.

It was Mary's sister Sarah's request in 1832 for admission to Prudence Crandall's Canterbury academy for girls that touched off a period of soul-searching for Crandall. Crandall carefully considered Sarah's request, consulting with the Harris family and notable abolitionists such as Garrison before closing her female academy and reopening it as a school reserved for girls of color. The decision led to a firestorm of protest against Crandall from her white neighbors, culminating in a strict new racist law in Connecticut that prohibited local schools from providing education to out-of-state Black residents without explicit approval by local authorities.

Mary Harris, along with her sister Sarah, attended Crandall's school for a time, before harassment, vandalism, and the new law forced the school to close and Crandall to permanently vacate Connecticut. While Sarah Harris's dreams of a teaching career never came to fruition, at least two of her sisters did lead classrooms. Mary taught in several communities, both before and after she married, and sister Olive also led classrooms when Mary taught in the seacoast city of New London.

Just a few years after the Crandall affair, Williams was teaching and living in Norwich, in a neighborhood where a Black community thrived, and where the Harrises had lived for many years. Mary and Pelleman were married on April 13, 1845, according to marriage records from the town of Canterbury. He was active in abolitionist circles, and in 1849, served as president of the Connecticut Convention of Colored Men.

They would have three children—Arthur, Pellemina, and Mirabella—and Arthur would continue the family's legacy in education. Pelleman and Mary's teaching careers apparently necessitated frequent moves. Throughout the antebellum period, state and federal census records show them living at various times in New Haven, Connecticut; New York City; and Norwich. The 1855 New York census listed them as living with their children in the city's fifth ward on the Lower West Side of Manhattan, along with Mary's brother Lloyd Garrison (named after the famed abolitionist), and a two-year-old boy named Clay Harris. Pelleman is listed as working as a teacher and Mary as a housekeeper.

By 1860 Mary and Pelleman were back in Norwich. He was forty-five at the time, and she was forty-two. Son Arthur was fourteen, and daughters Mirabella and Pellemina were eleven and six, respectively. The Williams family had done relatively well for themselves financially by this time. At a time when most Blacks didn't, or couldn't—because of local restrictions—own property, census records show the Williams family owned real estate valued at $500 (about $19,500 in 2025) and had a personal estate valued at $1,500.

Early in the Civil War, however, the Williams family was presented with an exciting and tantalizing opportunity that would allow them to make significant and unprecedented contributions to the education of children of color. They uprooted their lives in a major way to follow this dream.

Federal forces in 1862 took control of New Orleans, a strategic Mississippi River port city in the heart of the South, creating a kind of oasis of freedom surrounded by slave territory. The occupation of New Orleans held the promise of an end to slavery, and an increase in the number of people of color coming to the city, seeking the joys of freedom and opportunities for education. Groups such as the American

Missionary Association began to actively recruit teachers from Northern states to come to the Crescent City to teach Black children.

For Williams and his wife, the goals to which they had dedicated their lives finally appeared within reach. While New Orleans had long had a large population of free Blacks dating back to its time under French rule, it also was located in the heart of an area where slaves had endured some of the most brutal treatment in an overall violent and dehumanizing system. Located near large sugar plantations notorious for their inhumane treatment of enslaved people, New Orleans in the hands of federal troops brimmed with hope and promise for people of color.

As the Civil War raged, shortly after Abraham Lincoln issued the Emancipation Proclamation in 1863, the Williams family undertook the perilous journey to New Orleans. There, they would use their classroom leadership expertise to teach. They also immersed themselves in other efforts to improve life for people of color.

Despite the optimism no doubt running high among the Williams family and those who were like-minded about the potential for freedmen, most of the white community in New Orleans despised the occupation by Union troops. They were far from happy with the infiltration of Northern teachers—both white and those of color—who came to teach Black students. Racial tensions and even violence against Blacks were not uncommon, and the Williams family would see racially motivated arson fires destroy schools with which they were associated. Such tragedies certainly must have been a vivid reminder for them of the events of the 1830s in Canterbury, Connecticut.

The work itself also was challenging, to say the least. One 1865 letter to the heads of the American Missionary Association—written by Josiah Beardsley, and now part of the association archives at The *Amistad* Center at Tulane University—detailed some of the conditions. None of the students even knew the alphabet when he began his job, Beardsley wrote, and classroom discipline was a foreign concept to them. "Dress, habits and appearance of the scholars were far from neat and attractive," he wrote.

Overcrowding in classrooms also led to frequent disputes. Beardsley wrote that there could be as many as 150 to 200 children in a room, and each day could see two or three "severe and bloody" fights among students. Still, he also noted that they were eager and able to learn. "I did not suppose it reasonable to believe that a people who had been the subject of oppression, generation after generation, would manifest as great [an] aptness in learning" as those who had not toiled in bondage, he wrote in his letter.

And, at least at first, the progress was impressive. A January 1866 letter from the Board of Education for Freedmen (also held in The *Amistad* Center archives of the association) noted that an astounding fifty thousand freedmen learned to read in two years. The general superintendent of Education of Freedmen and Refugees noted, however, that the schools could be conducted for less money by using "colored" teachers—who presumably would be paid lower salaries—than by hiring white teachers.

Letters written to the missionary association that are part of The *Amistad* Center collection show that many Northern churches, individuals, and schools sent clothing, books, and other supplies for the new scholars, and many residents requested positions as teachers. Support also was sent by those in authority in the North. Governor William Buckingham of Connecticut, for example, who hailed from the Harrises' hometown of Norwich, demonstrated his support for the efforts of teaching freed slaves by sending a donation of $250, which he indicated would sustain a teacher in the colored regiment for a year.

Besides teaching younger students, the Williamses, who established their homestead at 1438 Euterpe Street, in what is today the Lower Garden District, also were integral to the establishment of the first institution of higher education for students of color in New Orleans—Straight University. While the university did not have a very long history, and was merged to become Dillard University in 1934, when it was established in 1868, Pelleman was named the head of the Normal School there, while Mary headed the English department.

Straight University was established originally on the Esplanade, in a neighborhood where many free Blacks had lived for generations. In 1877, after the Williamses had already moved on to teaching positions outside of Straight, a racially motivated arson fire destroyed the main university building, and Straight relocated to Canal Street, a dividing line between the traditional Creole neighborhoods of the city and more Anglo or American neighborhoods.

Buildings at Straight University, the first institution of higher education for students of color in New Orleans. Pelleman and Mary Williams were integral to its founding. This image is from the years after the Williamses were no longer teaching there. (The Historic New Orleans Collection, Williams Research Center)

Rules at Straight were strict, according to documents from the early days of the institution archived in the Historic New Orleans Collection. Students rose at 6:15 a.m., had breakfast, and attended services at the chapel daily. After a full day of classes, they studied for two hours each evening, and went to bed just before 10:00 p.m. A leaflet detailing the university's rules also warned students against conversing with members of the opposite sex, and indicated that they must abstain from using tobacco or alcohol. According to an 1883–1884 leaflet for the school: "It should be the aim and ambition of all to go out into the battlefield of life fully armed and equipped for the conflict."

Besides working in education, the Williams family also became entrenched in the New Orleans Black community in many other ways.

One was working to establish a new newspaper. A page-one article on May 13, 1865, in a publication called *The Colophon*, detailed plans to begin a new newspaper called *The Black Republican*. Professor P. M. Williams is listed as one of the organizers of this effort. A meeting was called for those who supported the plans to come together at St. Paul's Church on Liberty Street, with 6 Carondelet Street as the proposed location for the newspaper's offices.

"It will be printed in the English tongue," the promotion read, "the tongue that brought us freedom. Through this paper the poor as well as the rich, the frenchmen as well as the freemen, will be heard." The newspaper was as much an educational endeavor as an attempt to provide news and information. An article about the newspaper published on the website of the Bullock Museum in Austin, Texas, indicates *The Black Republican* was a weekly distributed on Saturdays. The newspaper's prospectus said the paper was "devoted to the religious, moral, social, political and material advancement of the colored people." Because so many in the Black community were still illiterate, the paper hosted meetings at its office during which the paper would be read out loud and free copies distributed.

The Williams family had established itself enough that other members of the Harris family joined them in the South. Mary's nephew George, Sarah's son, joined his aunt, uncle, and cousins in New Orleans, working as a journalist in the city before returning north to New York.

By the late 1870s, when Reconstruction ended and white authority again moved to restrict opportunities and progress for people of color, Pelleman Williams began teaching outside New Orleans. On January 4, 1879, the *Weekly Louisianian* reported, "Prof. P. M. Williams, principal of the colored Peabody School at Baton Rouge East, was in the city [New Orleans] during the holidays on a visit to his family. The Professor looks hale and hearty, and seems to be as deeply interested in the work of education as ever."

Shortly thereafter, he moved on from the Peabody School to teach at Strickland Plantation in St. Helena Parish, in the northern part of the state near the Mississippi state line. He ended up teaching until the day he died in St. Helena Parish, at the age of sixty-six. The death notice in the *Times-Picayune*, published on September 13, 1882, noted that Williams died on September 11, and was a resident of New Orleans for twenty years.

A dedication to education continued in the Williams family even after Pelleman's death. Mary and Pelleman's son Arthur and Arthur's wife Sylvanie also were longtime, respected teachers in New Orleans. The New Orleans City Directory of 1890–1891 listed Arthur as principal of the Fisk School for boys and Sylvanie as a teacher. The Fisk School became known for two of its famous students—Louis Armstrong and Charles "Buddy" Bolden, both jazz icons. Sarah's son George also is listed as a teacher at this time.

In the book *Music and Some Highly Musical People: Remarkable Musicians of the Colored Race*, written by James M. Trotter and published in 1881, Professor A. P. Williams is recognized. He is listed as a vocalist, pianist, and teacher of vocal and instrumental music, and is said to have received his instruction from his father. A. P. Williams is listed as an instructor of a grammar school in New Orleans, and his wife as principal of one of the largest colored schools in the city.

It seems fitting that Mary died in 1900, shortly after the century that had held much promise for people of color but ultimately ended with setbacks, racist attacks, and the emergence of degrading and strict Jim Crow laws. The *Times-Picayune* on May 16, 1900, reported Mary's death at age eighty-four, saying she had been a teacher in New Orleans for thirty-six years. Mary was interred in the Girod Street Cemetery, where her husband was buried, although years later the cemetery became so neglected and vandalized it was deconsecrated, and Mary and Pelleman's remains were moved.

The teaching tradition of the Williams family continued into the early years of the twentieth century. Arthur P. Williams and his wife also both remained in the profession until their deaths. Arthur's *Times-Picayune* 1920 obituary reported he was seventy-four at the time of his death, and a resident of New Orleans for fifty-seven years. A paper called the *New Orleans States* reported the death under the headline, "Arthur Williams, Veteran Teacher, Dies in Harness." The short article reports he died at the family home on Euterpe Street, and said of him, "He is one of the best known negro educators in the South." He was interred at the Lafayette Cemetery Number 2.

Now, the family legacy of education remained with Sylvanie. She was a graduate of the Peabody Normal School and later became its principal, and only teacher. According to information from The Historic New Orleans Collection, she became the first principal of the Thomy Lafon School for students of color in 1896 and saw the school destroyed by a fire during a race riot in 1900. She led an effort to rebuild, and the school reopened about six years later.

She also founded the local Phillis Wheatley Club associated with the National Association of Colored Women. The club opened a nursing school for women of color and a free medical clinic. In addition, it advocated for suffrage for women of color, and in 1915, Williams led the effort that funded the first public playground for children of color in New Orleans.

Sylvanie retired shortly before her death in 1921, just a year after her husband's death. Her legacy and work in education continues in the city. An elementary school in New Orleans was named in her honor in 1971.

Maine
Racism Common in State Where Slavery Was Abolished Relatively Early

In 1794, a Black man named Benjamin Darling purchased a small island in Casco Bay, off Midcoast Maine. His descendants later inhabited several of the islands in that region, and by the time of the Civil War, family members were living on the forty-two-acre Malaga Island. A mixed-race community of poor fishing families expanded on the island through the years. There were twenty-seven people living on Malaga by 1880, and forty by 1900.

Despite their long roots in Maine, by the early twentieth century the Malaga Island inhabitants became victims of the still-widespread racism in the country. In addition, authorities worried that the rude and humble houses of the island residents would discourage tourism, upon which the state's economy was increasingly dependent. Newspapers of the era, along with some local residents, perpetuated the point of view that the island residents were lazy drunkards. They agitated for forcibly removing the islanders from the area.

In that atmosphere, the Malaga Island community was ordered to leave their longtime homes by July 1, 1912. Along with the living residents, the bodies of dead residents were exhumed and the island burial ground relocated to the mainland. The sad saga of Malaga Island demonstrates the length and breadth of racial disdain, not just in Maine, but throughout the United States. Long after hard-fought battles against slavery were won and certain basic civil rights granted to Black citizens, racism prevailed, and influenced decision-making by authorities for many years.

The shameful treatment of Malaga Island residents belies the fact that people of color have a long and distinctive history in Maine. The 2006 book *Maine's Visible Black History: The First Chronicle of its People*, by H. H. Price and Gerald E. Talbot, indicates that Blacks lived in the territory that is now the state of Maine for as long as did whites of European descent. Many of the Black settlers to the area were mariners, and some contemporary Black Maine families can trace their ancestry to Cape Verde, which carried on commercial trade with Maine from the early colonial era.

In 1652, the area that is now Maine became part of the colony of Massachusetts. When Massachusetts abolished slavery in 1783, the institution also was abolished in the territory that is now Maine. Still, slavery was not uncommon in Maine during the eighteenth century, when many of Maine's wealthier residents owned enslaved people to work as house servants or in farming and marine trades.

William Pepperrell of Kittery, a merchant who was among the wealthiest men in the American colonies, enslaved several people. One sad incident in 1719 illustrates the general acceptance of slavery, as well as the callousness with which wealthy white colonists viewed people of color. Pepperrell was bringing five enslaved people from the West Indies to Maine, but four of them died at sea and one died just three weeks after her arrival in Kittery. The deaths were matter-of-factly reported by Pepperrell and, judging by his correspondence, only the financial losses their deaths caused seemed to be of any concern to him.

Throughout the time before statehood, there were Black residents, both free and enslaved, living in many communities in Maine. While their numbers might have been small in comparison to Black communities in places such as Boston and New York City, people of color from Maine made numerous notable achievements. They served their country in the military, including in the American Revolution, and worked hard at a variety of professions that were open to them, including as mariners, teachers, business owners, farmers, and builders.

Maine's very existence as a state is inextricably intertwined with the country's bitter debate over slavery during the nineteenth century. Maine separated from Massachusetts and approved a state constitution in 1819, a constitution that allowed for Black suffrage in the state. Maine would not be admitted to the Union as the twenty-third state until the following year, however, and then only as part of the so-called Missouri Compromise, which kept the balance of slave-owning and free states equal by admitting both Maine and Missouri—one free and one slave-owning—to the Union at the same time.

While Maine was admitted as a free state, leading many contemporaries to conclude that the predominantly white population overwhelmingly supported abolition, historians estimate that in reality, half the state's population was sympathetic to the pro-slavery cause. Still, organized abolitionist groups were established in Maine, and the first anti-slavery society in the state was formed in 1833. Abolitionist lecturers also came to Maine, but they were sometimes met by a hostile populace, and most religious organizations in the state maintained a hands-off approach to the topic of slavery.

Some notable abolitionists were from Maine, including Abraham Lincoln's first vice president, Hannibal Hamlin. Henry Wadsworth Longfellow, the famous poet who held anti-slavery sentiments, was born in Portland, and was a graduate of Bowdoin College. Harriet Beecher Stowe was living in Brunswick, Maine, when she penned the seminal anti-slavery novel *Uncle Tom's Cabin*.

It was largely the Black community and Black mariners, however, especially in places such as Portland and Bangor, who worked the most diligently to promote the anti-slavery cause in Maine. Many also were active conductors on the Underground Railroad. Maine had a sizable network of safe houses, where self-emancipated slaves traveling to freedom in Canada could find respite, get warm clothing and food, and maybe even a makeover to their hair to help disguise their appearance.

Even after the Civil War finally decided the question of slavery in the United States, racism remained entrenched throughout the country. Maine outlawed interracial marriage and imposed barriers to voting. In 1893, it made literacy a condition of voting, and although the law was aimed primarily at keeping newer immigrants from the polls, it also disenfranchised residents of color disproportionately.

In contemporary times, Maine historians and residents have worked to reclaim the state's important Black history. In 2007, the Portland Freedom Trail was established to help keep alive the stories of its notable Black residents from the past. Guided Black history tours are also regularly offered in Portland.

Among the sites on the trail is the Abyssinian Meeting House at 73 Newbury Street, the third-oldest African American meetinghouse still standing in the country. The building required extensive renovation when it was acquired by the Committee to Restore the Abyssinian in 1998. It was the first site in Maine to be listed on the National Park Service's National Underground Railroad Network to Freedom. It is also a City of Portland landmark and is listed on the National Register of Historic Places.

First Parish Church, Unitarian Universalist in Portland, Maine, where leading abolitionist William Lloyd Garrison addressed a crowd of some two thousand people on his first anti-slavery tour of Maine in 1832. (Author's Collection)

Charles Frederick Eastman
Foremost Conductor of the Underground Railroad

When Charles Frederick Eastman died in 1880, his obituary in the *Portland Daily Press* noted that he was a "well known and respected colored citizen." The obituary also provided some details about his life: "Mr. Eastman was born in this city [Portland] fifty-nine years ago, and by his industry accumulated quite a nice little property. He was self-educated and a great reader. During his later years he accumulated a large collection of valuable books, making a library of no mean proportions." The obituary reports that Eastman was a taxidermist who preserved rare birds and small animals and created a small museum of these preserved creatures in his home. He married Harriet W. Stephenson in November 1842. The couple had nine children between 1843 and 1866.

While these facts paint a picture of an interesting, somewhat eclectic person who was undoubtedly a high-achieving individual, given that at this time many Black Americans were illiterate largely because of barriers to education put in their path, the most important passage in the obituary likely is this one: "During the enforcement of the fugitive slave law Mr. Eastman was one of the regular 'conductors' of the 'Underground Railroad,' and no man did more for the poor fugitives escaping from slavery than he." A second obituary published in the *Portland Daily Advertiser* notes: "For years he labored for the emancipation of his own race, and when that was accomplished he gave his time to the building up of his church and the education and training of his children."

Beyond these published obituaries, the public record on Eastman is scarce, despite his being a leading and essential member of Portland's Black community, and one who contributed both his time and financial resources to support causes that would improve the lives of Black Americans.

Eastman was born and lived in the seacoast city of Portland, Maine. Little is known about his parents. As did many nineteenth-century Blacks, Eastman worked in several different capacities to earn his living. Unlike many of his contemporaries, however, Eastman was financially successful. According to the entry marking his home on the Portland Freedom Trail, Eastman was a mariner and secondhand clothing dealer. He also owned his own barbershop and invested in and sold various pieces of real estate. Many of those who dealt in secondhand clothes kept warm clothing available to give to those escaping slavery, as they were traveling from hotter climates to the much chillier North.

Eastman also operated a hack service, the contemporary equivalent of a taxi service. Operating such a business—just as Reuben Ruby did, also in Portland—would have provided a perfect front for transporting those who were fleeing slavery. (Reuben Ruby is profiled later in this section.) In addition, Eastman's barbershop provided a place where self-emancipated slaves could get makeovers in the form of different hairstyles, or even wigs, to make them less likely to be recognized by anyone who might have been familiar with them during their enslavement.

The very nature of the Underground Railroad means it had to operate clandestinely. Because of this, little hard evidence or primary records exist of many of the so-called "conductors" or the stops visited by self-emancipating slaves on their route toward safety and freedom. Still, there is much anecdotal evidence that Eastman was integral to the Underground Railroad in Maine, and he is included in *The Underground Railroad: An Encyclopedia of People, Places and Operations*, a 2008 book written by Mary Ellen Snodgrass.

Maine played a vital role in the Underground Railroad network. Many escaping slaves arrived in ports such as Portland and were assisted along their way by a network of Blacks, as well as white residents sympathetic to their cause. Many Black mariners worked aboard all types of commercial ships, and escaping slaves often were aided by them while on the water. Once in Maine, they would find a network of seventy-five or more safe houses located throughout the state.

Many escaping slaves made Northern states that had abolished slavery their final destination. After the 1850 Fugitive Slave Act passed, however, that law made it easier for slave hunters to grab up the formerly enslaved, forcing Northern officials and residents to help return these unfortunate souls to slavery. This meant most escaping slaves after this point headed instead to Canada. Even though an estimated half of Maine's population supported slavery in the mid-nineteenth century, the abolitionist network was strong and prolific enough that an estimated 140,000 former slaves were helped on their way to Canada via the state's Underground Railroad network.

Besides his direct work assisting escaping slaves, Eastman also supported his community through his active work for the Abyssinian church. He provided the church with much-needed funding during times when it was struggling financially, and his name appears frequently in church records. In addition, he assisted in the operations of the school that was run from the church.

The Abyssinian Religious Society was established in 1828. The estimated six hundred members of Portland's Black community were disgruntled by the second-rate treatment they received at the predominantly white Second Congregational Church, and so formed their own worship community. The building also served as a meeting hall and community center for Black residents. Fiery anti-slavery speeches were given there, including by well-known abolitionists such as William Lloyd Garrison and Frederick Douglass.

His *Portland Daily Press* obituary notes that Eastman "was a member of the Newbury Street church, and it was by his wise counsel and liberal giving that the church was sustained when the poverty of the colored people would have compelled them to close up the church."

The Eastman family's affiliation with the church and its dedication to community service apparently continued in subsequent generations. An 1898 newspaper notice about Charles Frederick Eastman Jr.'s funeral reported that the church was filled for his final services. "Mr. Perkins [a minister] referred feelingly to the services of Mr. Eastman to Fraternity House, and to the respect, esteem and friendship he and his family had won during their connection with the institution." Fraternity House sponsored various charities and community groups and events in the city.

Eighteen years earlier, the elder Eastman's *Portland Daily Press* obituary noted, "As a man he was looked up to by the people of his own race, and respected by all who knew him. For years he labored for the emancipation of his own race, and when that was accomplished he gave his time to the building up of his church and the education and training of his children. The same faith in God that always characterized his actions through life sustained him through a painful sickness of more than a year, and yesterday morning his life, full of good deeds, ended. He leaves a wife and six children."

Eastman, along with a dozen of his relatives, is buried in Portland's Evergreen Cemetery. In 1862, Eastman purchased an expensive burial plot in that cemetery in a prestigious and more scenic section, close to decorative pavilions and bridges. The section was traditionally reserved for whites.

Although greatly altered from the nineteenth century, the building on the right on Newbury Street is a house where George Eastman lived, just two buildings away from the Abyssinian Meeting House. Eastman was an active member of the congregation, and provided the church with financial support. (Author's Collection)

Portland Freedom Trail marker noting the Eastman House on Newbury Street. (Author's Collection)

Robert Benjamin Lewis
Author of First Afrocentric History Book

Search this work with care and candor;
Every line and page you read
Will brighten all the truths of Scripture,
Proved by history—plain indeed.

These words are written on the cover page of the 1844 edition of a book titled *Light and Truth*, written by Robert Benjamin Lewis, a native of Maine. Also on the cover page is a subtitle that calls the book the "Universal History of the Colored and the Indian Race." Lewis was an ethnographer, inventor, and entrepreneur, and his book is counted as the first Afrocentric history book. It details the great lives, civilizations, and moments in history associated with people of color.

This building now housing the Lucky Cheetah restaurant in Portland, Maine, is where Robert Benjamin Lewis's *Light and Truth* was published. In Lewis's time, the building was the home of the printing firm of Daniel Clement Colesworthy. (Author's Collection)

The introduction to the book, written by a publishing committee of "colored gentlemen," points out the abuse and mistreatment of both Blacks and Native Americans by the white-dominated society at the time. "In this country, where the former [Blacks] are subjected to the deepest degradation—where every variety of persecution is measured out to this unfortunate race, it is highly expedient that 'Light and Truth' should be promulgated, in order that oppressors shall not consider it an indispensable duty to trample upon the weak and defenseless."

The introduction continues: "In a large portion of this country, men, women and children belonging to this race, are held as articles of merchandize [sic] by the whites; the iron heart of gain hath forgotten every sacred and social relation, while, at its expense, millions have perished on the cursed rack."

As the debate over slavery in the United States heated up during the nineteenth century, rhetoric on both sides also escalated. Abolitionists appealed to Americans' Christian faith and their sense of decency in their calls for immediate or even gradual abolition. Anti-abolitionists, on the other hand, often used passages from the Bible to argue that slavery had been employed since ancient times, and so should be seen as part of the natural order of life. They also used pseudoscience to help justify the institution, often arguing there were innate biological characteristics that "proved" the inferiority of people of color.

Lewis, through this written history, didn't resort to emotional appeals, but instead stated in matter-of-fact terms the great achievements of Black- and Native-controlled civilizations dating back hundreds and hundreds of years.

What is known about Lewis's life is rather sketchy. He was born in 1802 in Pittston, Maine, in an area that is now part of the city of Gardiner, located just south of Augusta. His father was a Native American from either the Mohegan or Pequot tribe in Connecticut. His mother was of African descent. Her father was kidnapped from Africa as a child and bought in the United States by a wealthy Boston physician who also was a land developer in Maine.

It's likely Lewis spent some time working at sea, and his descendants later said he served in the War of 1812. Because he was still a child at that time, he may have served as a ship's cabin boy.

Many New England men of color became mariners. Ships' crews were generally diverse, and crew members were afforded respect and treatment commensurate with their skill levels. While serving aboard a ship during the age of sail was lonely, dangerous, and brutal work in many ways, the sea was a place where men of color might escape the racial barriers and prejudices that prevented them from working in so many land-based professions in America.

There is evidence Lewis moved around considerably when not at sea. In Maine, he lived in Portland, Hallowell, and Bath at various times. He married first to Wealthia Ann Jones in New York City in 1828. Then, in 1835, in Boston, he married Mary Freeman Huston. His second marriage produced at least three sons and seven daughters, with sources disagreeing on exact numbers.

Also as was common with some men of color, Lewis worked at numerous types of jobs to earn a living and support his large family. He worked a variety of odd jobs as a day laborer and also as a whitewasher, in addition to going to sea.

Lewis clearly was educated, and he made good use of his knowledge. He earned three patents, an accomplishment that was rare for men of color in the early nineteenth century. In June 1836, he received a US patent for a machine called a "hair picker." Lewis wrote in his patent application that the machine would be useful for picking oakum, a natural rope-type fiber used extensively aboard ships for caulking and sealing. The machine was a common item in Maine shipyards for years afterward.

Lewis's second patent was awarded in 1840 for a machine called a "feather renovator." This device was used to help clean and dry feathers at a time when they were used extensively as decorations on women's hats and in other fashions.

Finally, he received a patent in 1841 for an improvement to large brushes used for whitewashing. The invention allowed bristles to be replaced in the brushes instead of needing to buy a new brush if only some of its bristles were worn out.

Another invention of Lewis's was not patented, but was a product he sold for many years. He called it "Lewis' Arabian Hair Oil." As did many purveyors of homemade and questionable toiletry products and medicines in this time period, Lewis apparently marketed his hair oil by making fairly far-fetched claims about its efficacy. Advertisements in Maine newspapers claimed that Lewis had secured the formula from an Arabian, and that the oil would prevent hair loss and make the hair grow especially long and thick. He reportedly wore his own hair quite long to illustrate the potency of his claims.

Even with all of these achievements, Lewis's greatest contribution to the cause of racial equality was his *Light and Truth*, which he originally wrote simply as a way to earn some money. It first was published as four 100-page pamphlets that he sold for 25 cents each. He traveled extensively, peddling the pamphlets that told a history of people of color at odds with the pseudoscience being simultaneously peddled by pro-slavery advocates, claiming Blacks were inherently less intelligent and created specifically for work as enslaved laborers.

The pamphlets were later joined together into a single volume and the book was reprinted several times. Lewis was counting on the book to sell at a brisker rate than did the pamphlets, but became frustrated with the effort. He then marketed the book himself. In the May 13, 1853, edition of *Frederick Douglass' Paper*, he sought help to publish a 1,600-page version of the book that he said would "remove the prejudices from whites against the Colored and Indian people in the United States."

Ultimately, Lewis grew disillusioned by efforts to gain more civil rights for Americans of color. Like other Black activists of the nineteenth century, Lewis believed that white Americans would never view or treat Blacks as their equals, and felt the only solution would be for Americans of color to emigrate overseas.

With that in mind, he traveled to Port-au-Prince, the capital of the Black republic of Haiti in 1857, to investigate whether it would be a suitable place to resettle his family. Unfortunately, he was not there long before he contracted yellow fever.

Lewis died in February 1858 and is buried in Haiti, a place where he dreamed Black Americans might live without the everyday harassment and barriers to success put in their way by racism in the United States.

Reuben Ruby

Abolitionist and Founder of the Abyssinian Church

By 1832, there was growing public sentiment that slavery in the United States must end. Despite this, Maine, which had been a state for only twelve years at that point, did not yet have any abolitionist organizations in place.

William Lloyd Garrison, one of the country's leading white abolitionists and publisher of the anti-slavery newspaper *The Liberator*, traveled to Maine in an effort to launch an abolitionist movement there. It was an action the state's Black community was especially eager to establish.

Garrison headed to the seaside community of Portland, where a substantial number of free Blacks lived, and where many enslaved people seeking freedom arrived on boats, seeking their first Northern US experience. He spent some of his time there being squired around the community by a hack driver and activist named Reuben Ruby. Garrison wrote that Ruby was "a colored gentleman held in much esteem in this city." Ruby was a primary driver behind the abolition movement in Maine, along with advocacy for equal rights for the free Black population in the state.

Besides the tour of Portland, Ruby also invited Garrison to his own home for a night of entertainment. Garrison later described the experience of meeting "twenty colored gentlemen of good intelligence and reputable character." He further wrote, "As a mark of their respect for my person and gratitude for my labors, I shall long cherish it in my memory; and I beg them to accept this public acknowledgment of their kindness as some evidence of appreciation." While in Portland, Garrison spoke to a large group of Black residents at the Abyssinian Meeting House that Ruby had helped found. Inspired by Garrison's speech, Ruby soon joined with a group of white Portland residents to establish one of the state's first anti-slavery societies.

Ruby was born in 1798 in Gray, Maine, a town located about fifteen miles northwest of Portland at a time when Maine was still part of Massachusetts. Ruby's father was an enslaved person whose roots were in northern Africa. Ruby experienced personal tragedy in his life: He was married three times and widowed twice. His first wife died just six years after the couple married in 1821. Shortly after, Ruby moved to Portland.

Ruby was a young man in his twenties when he moved from Gray to Portland. There he established a hack business, essentially a taxi company. It was the first such business in the state of Maine. A newspaper advertisement for the business shows an illustration of a coach drawn by two horses and text indicating how the public could locate his transportation service: "Reuben Ruby informs the public that he has two good Coaches, one or the other of which may generally be found at his old Stand, at the Elm Tavern, where he will be happy to attend to any calls which are made upon him. Every attention will be paid to accommodate those who wish to be conveyed to different parts of the City, or elsewhere. His residence is the second house on the east side of Preble Street, from the head, where he may be found at any time in the night."

Now the Casco apartments, this is the Portland site of the Elm Tavern, where Reuben Ruby operated a hack stand. (Author's Collection)

Being found in the night may have been especially important for him, as he was frequently called on to help transport to safety those who were escaping slavery. Ruby became known as one of the area's foremost conductors on the Underground Railroad.

In the late 1820s Ruby was instrumental in the founding of the Abyssinian Religious Society after voicing his distress over the poor treatment of Black parishioners by the white-dominated churches in the city. In 1826, he and five other men wrote a letter to a local newspaper severely criticizing this second-class treatment. Rather than wait for the white church congregants to change their ways, the Black community decided to establish its own house of worship.

The Abyssinian church on Newbury Street, one of the oldest Black churches still standing in the United States. (Author's Collection)

Ruby donated the land and also was a major financial contributor to the church's construction. It was the first Black church established in Portland, as well as in Maine, and it became a hub of religious services and social gatherings for the community, as well as for meetings to discuss the Underground Railroad and abolitionist advocacy. Many slaves escaping servitude in the South were sheltered in the church. The church also sponsored a school and provided employment assistance and temperance support to the Black community.

In 1834, Ruby was one of four delegates from Portland at the first convention of the Maine Anti-Slavery Society. In 1837, he was a member of the executive committee of the New England Temperance Convention.

In that same year of 1837, Ruby and his family left Maine and moved to New York City, but by 1849, Ruby was lured to California by the prospect of striking it rich in the gold rush. Ruby was among just a minute fraction of the thousands of prospectors who actually succeeded in the California gold fields. He then returned to Portland, where he remained for the rest of his life. In Portland, he invested some of his wealth in a variety of business ventures, including a restaurant and a watchmaking shop. Ruby died in 1878, and is buried in Portland.

The Abyssinian Meeting House survived the Great Fire of 1866 in Portland because Ruby's son, a firefighter, doused it in water so the building would better resist the flames. Some ten thousand people were left homeless because of that fire.

The Abyssinian Meeting House closed in 1917 and was converted to an apartment building. It was later abandoned. The City of Portland assumed ownership of the building because of back taxes owed. In 1998, the Committee to Restore the Abyssinian bought the property and began working to restore it. The building is now a designated city landmark and listed on the National Register of Historic Places.

John Brown Russwurm
Pioneering Black Journalist

Today a busy intersection in downtown Portland at the edge of Casco Bay, John Brown Russwurm would have arrived in Maine near this site. He lived in the city with his white father and stepmother in the early 1800s. (Author's Collection)

On the front page of the March 16, 1827, inaugural edition of *Freedom's Journal*, the country's first Black-run newspaper, the editors provided a lengthy description of the publication's mission:

> *The peculiarities of the Journal render it important that we should advertise to the world the motives by which we are actuated, and the objects which we contemplate.*
>
> *We wish to plead our own cause. Too long have others spoken for us. Too long has the publick been deceived by misrepresentations in things which concern us dearly, though in the estimation of some mere trifles; for though there are many in society who exercise towards us benevolent feelings; still (with sorrow we confess it) there are others who make it their business to enlarge upon the least trifle, which tends to the discredit of any person of colour; and pronounce anathemas and denounce our whole body for the misconduct of this guilty one.*
>
> *We are aware that there [are] many instances of vice among us, but we avow that it is because no one has taught its subjects to be virtuous; many instances of poverty because no sufficient efforts accommodated to minds contracted by slavery, and deprived of early education have been made, to teach them how to husband their hard earnings, and to secure to themselves comforts.*

Published in New York City, the *Journal* began its run the same year the state abolished slavery, representing a momentous change in the world of American journalism that generally ignored any news or information for, or about, Blacks. Not only was it written, edited, and published by Black residents, it also contained articles that went well beyond advocating for abolition and civil rights for Americans of color. It also published inspirational profiles of notable Blacks, such as Paul Cuffe and Phyllis Wheatley, along with day-to-day news such as birth, death, and marriage announcements, articles that advocated for improved education for Americans of color, and general news and information important to the Black community.

As its mission statement made clear, the newspaper was evidence the community wanted to tell its story in its own words, and not through the too-often biased and bigoted lens of the majority white community, nor through the words of well-meaning white abolitionists who could not fully comprehend the everyday heartaches endured by Blacks living with endemic racism.

Samuel E. Cornish and John Brown Russwurm served as the paper's senior and junior editors, respectively. The paper was published for only two years, and Cornish and Russwurm parted ways over a deep disagreement about the colonization movement that advocated for the relocation of Black Americans to Africa, Haiti, or other predominantly Black areas. Although the paper initially criticized colonization, Russwurm grew to believe in the movement as a way for Blacks to form their own thriving communities without having to constantly fight racial prejudice. He would move to Africa himself in his later years.

Besides the remarkable achievement of being one of the first American Black newspapermen, Russwurm's life was notable for many other reasons. His white father embraced him and gave him the Russwurm surname, unlike the vast majority of whites who fathered children by women of color. Russwurm was also loved and considered a valuable member of the family of his white stepmother in Portland, Maine. Russwurm was highly educated and was the first Black graduate of Bowdoin College in Brunswick, Maine. He also was one of the first Black American scholars to join a fraternity while at college.

Russwurm was born in Jamaica on October 1, 1799. His father, John Russwurm, was an American merchant. Little is known definitively about Russwurm's mother. Many sources say she was enslaved, but others say she was a free Creole woman, likely of mixed African and European descent. When he was about eight years old, his father sent him to Quebec to be educated. At this point he was known as "John Brown," as his father had not yet given him the Russwurm surname.

By 1812, Russwurm's father had moved back to Portland, Maine. There, he married a woman named Susan Blanchard, who apparently encouraged her husband to rename his son John Brown Russwurm. John Brown Russwurm was brought into the blended Russwurm–Blanchard family, where he was treated equally, and lovingly. His stepmother had children by a previous marriage, so the child now cohabited with step-siblings.

Russwurm's father and stepmother had been married only three years when the elder Russwurm died. His stepmother again remarried, to a man named William Hawes. John Brown Russwurm continued to be a valued member of the family, however.

Russwurm was sent by the family to continue his education at the coeducational boarding school Hebron Academy, located about forty miles north of Portland. In 1824, he was admitted to Bowdoin College, where Henry Wadsworth Longfellow and Nathaniel Hawthorne were among his classmates. Russwurm became the first Black student admitted to the Athenaean Society, a literary and debating organization.

While Russwurm was apparently a solid student, he was socially isolated because of his race. He lived off campus, and although he sometimes was visited by Hawthorne and other classmates, he didn't venture out to visit them. Still, he was accepted enough that he gave a graduation speech when he earned his bachelor's degree, as was the tradition at the time, and one denied other Black scholars at other institutions of higher education. As he became the first Black graduate from Bowdoin, he spoke about the Black republic of Haiti and its future prospects, a topic fraught with controversy. Many white Americans were terrified about the fact that a slave uprising had led to the Haitian revolution, something they feared might be replicated in the United States. The United States did not formally recognize Haiti until 1862.

After graduation, Russwurm went to Boston to teach in the school for Black children that would become the Abiel Smith School. In 1827, he moved to New York City, where he met numerous elite members of the Black community, including Cornish, who was the minister of the first Black Presbyterian church.

Russwurm and Cornish soon turned their attention to publishing *Freedom's Journal*. The paper was published weekly, and a yearly subscription cost $3. Between fourteen and forty-four agents sold subscriptions to the paper in various regions. The paper was delivered to subscribers in eleven states and the District of Columbia, as well as overseas to Haiti, Europe, and Canada.

In the inaugural edition, more of the paper's mission was explained in the front-page editorial:

> *It is our earnest wish to make our Journal a medium of intercourse between our brethren in the different states of this great confederacy; that through its columns an expression of our sentiments, on many interesting subjects which concern us, may be offered to the publick; that plans which apparently are beneficial may be candidly discussed and properly weighed; if worthy, receive our cordial approbation; if not, our marked disapprobation.*
>
> *Useful knowledge of every kind, and every thing that relates to Africa, shall find a ready admission into our columns; and as that vast continent becomes daily more known we trust that many things will come to light, proving that the natives of it are neither so ignorant nor stupid as they have generally been supposed to be.*
>
> *And while these important subjects shall occupy the columns of the FREEDOM'S JOURNAL, we would not be unmindful of our brethren who are still in the iron fetters of bondage. They are our kindred by all the ties of nature; and though but little can be effected by us, still let our sympathies be poured forth, and our prayers in their behalf ascend to Him who is able to succour them.*

John Brown Russwurm

Front page of the inaugural edition of *Freedom's Journal*. (Public Domain / Courtesy of Wikimedia Commons)

After Cornish resigned and Russwurm embraced the colonization movement, the paper lost appeal with its readers because many Black Americans opposed the concept of colonization. Russwurm, however, had grown disillusioned with efforts to persuade white Americans that slavery needed to be abolished and that Blacks were intellectually equal and deserving of civil rights. He had become convinced that Blacks would thrive and live a life free of racial bigotry only if they left the United States.

With the paper's subscription rates falling, Russwurm ceased publication of *Freedom's Journal* in March 1829 and temporarily moved back to Maine, where he earned a master's degree from Bowdoin. Russwurm then migrated to the American Colonization Society's colony of Liberia, and Cornish resumed publication of the newspaper, although he renamed it the *Rights of All* and did not support colonization.

For Russwurm, traveling to Africa was like a dream come true. On November 12, 1829, he arrived in Monrovia, Liberia, and assumed the position of superintendent of public schools. While there, he again turned to publishing, establishing the *Liberia Herald*, a newspaper especially focused on promoting education.

In 1833, when Russwurm was in his thirties, he married Sarah McGill, the daughter of Monrovia's lieutenant governor. The couple would have four children, and just one year before his death, Russwurm traveled back to Maine with two of his sons. He wanted them to be educated in Maine. They lived with his stepmother and attended North Yarmouth Academy.

In 1834, the Maryland State Colonization Society established a separate colony in Liberia, called Maryland. Russwurm became its governor in 1836, and remained in that position until his death. He proved to be an able leader and oversaw a growing, stable colony where he felt very much at home.

Russwurm died in 1851. A statue of him was erected in his burial spot at Cape Palmas as a tribute to his work in establishing a colony dedicated to allowing Black residents to realize their full human potential. Many years later, he also would be honored by his alma mater, when in 1970 Bowdoin named a house for him that now serves as a center for African American campus activities. In 2002, Molefi Kete Asante granted Russwurm a crowning posthumous achievement when he included Russwurm on his list of "100 Greatest African Americans."

MASSACHUSETTS
Leader in Abolitionist Thought and Action

Interior of the African Meeting House at the Museum of African American History on Boston's Black Heritage Trail, the birthplace of formal anti-slavery organizations in Massachusetts. (Author's Collection)

Just as Massachusetts played an integral part in fanning the flames of revolution that led to the North American British colonies becoming the United States of America, so, too, was Massachusetts a locus of anti-slavery activism in the nineteenth century that ultimately led to the Civil War and emancipation for all enslaved people of color in the country.

Boston was the home of the leading abolitionist newspaper, *The Liberator*, and ground zero in the country for radical abolitionist thought and action. With one of the country's largest communities of free Blacks—some two thousand people—Boston was a place where enslaved people escaping from the institution in the South could find shelter, food, and safety. It was a city where anti-slavery and vigilance groups aimed at protecting escaping slaves thrived, and where outspoken agitation for civil rights for people of color was not uncommon.

Yet, the paradox of anti-slavery sentiment and racism was alive in Massachusetts, just as in other states in the Northeast. Slavery was legal and commonplace in Massachusetts from the earliest days of European settlement, a time when most enslaved people were Native Americans whose communities were defeated and torn apart in violent skirmishes and wars with European settlers.

Just as in other places in New England, the Massachusetts economy was intertwined with the institution of slavery from the early colonial period. Mariners not only participated directly in the slave trade but also provided provisions to plantations in the West Indies that relied on enslaved labor. Distilleries in Boston relied on rum and enslaved labor from the Caribbean to operate. Later, the textile mills of Massachusetts were dependent on Southern cotton.

Massachusetts was among the earliest states to make slavery illegal. It also was among the first states where Black men could vote and where segregated schools were outlawed. Yet racism was also present and sometimes virulent in Massachusetts, as it was elsewhere. Leading abolitionist William Lloyd Garrison was attacked by a mob and only narrowly escaped with his life in 1835. Charlotte Forten frequently wrote in her journals about being shunned and isolated by her white classmates in Salem. Sarah Parker Remond was thrown down a flight of stairs after she and a companion tried to take the seats they had paid for in a choice location in a Boston theater. A violent, racially motivated melee broke out between sailors and a group of Blacks on Ann Street in Boston in 1843.

These incidents were not at odds with the beliefs held by many members of the white majority in America in the nineteenth century. They also were a continuation of long-accepted practices that strove to keep people of color subservient to and less than their white counterparts.

As early as the 1620s, British colonists began to enslave Native Americans. As the 1600s progressed, many of these earliest enslaved people came from the ranks of those captured in the Pequot War and King Philip's War. According to a City of Boston exhibit focused on slavery, the first enslaved Africans arrived in the city in 1638 aboard a vessel named *Desire*. By 1700, there were 1,000 enslaved Natives and Africans living in New England, and by 1720, there were more than 1,500 enslaved people living in Boston.

By the time of the Revolution, some enslaved people were being emancipated. Some earned their freedom by fighting with the Continental forces. Amid the revolutionary fervor, Blacks, too, yearned for freedom. Prince Hall, who fought in the American Revolution, was among a group of Black men who unsuccessfully petitioned the Massachusetts legislature in 1777, asking for the gradual abolition of slavery. He established the first Masonic lodge for men of color, which served as a mutual aid society for the Black community.

In 1780, Massachusetts adopted a constitution that included the words "All men are born free and equal, and have certain natural, essential, and unalienable rights." In several separate cases in the following years, the courts interpreted the constitution to mean that slavery would not be tolerated in the Commonwealth.

One of these cases is known as the Mum Bett case. Bett was enslaved by Colonel John Ashley in Berkshire County. Bett later said she had heard talk about the Declaration of Independence and the Massachusetts Constitution. She fled her enslavement, possibly after she tried to intervene during a heated encounter between her mistress and Bett's sister. Bett was struck with a hot shovel during the violent encounter.

When Ashley tried to force Bett's return to his household, a legal struggle ensued. In court, Bett's attorney argued that slavery was illegal in Massachusetts, and ultimately, the court agreed with him, setting Bett free. Yet, even then, many white residents throughout Massachusetts continued to keep enslaved people working in agriculture and as domestic help. Often, Black people who were enslaved, many of whom were illiterate, were unaware of the legal rulings and the move away from slavery in Massachusetts.

While Boston was clearly the focal point of abolitionist activity and home to a large number of activists, other towns and cities in Massachusetts also had Black communities that made their voices heard. Springfield and Salem had significant communities of color, for example. In Northampton, a utopian, racially integrated community called the Northampton Association of Education and Industry, located in the village of Florence, attracted the likes of abolitionists David Ruggles and Sojourner Truth.

New Bedford also had a large Black community. Its identity as a seacoast town, dependent on maritime trades like whaling, had long attracted residents of all racial backgrounds from around the globe. It was there that Frederick Douglass first made a home as a free man after escaping slavery in Maryland. Today, New Bedford has established Abolition Row Park to commemorate its Black and abolitionist history.

New Bedford is not the only place where Black history for decades was nearly forgotten, and is now reclaimed and celebrated. Other well-known sites in Massachusetts include a Boston Common monument honoring the Massachusetts 54th Regiment, the first Black regiment of the Civil War; the Museum of African American History, with campuses located in Boston and Nantucket; and Black heritage trails, monuments, and statues, all honoring these brave heroes of the fight to end slavery and to promote civil rights and racial equality.

Paul Cuffe

Mariner, Early Back-to-Africa Proponent, and Wealthy Businessman

Engraving of Paul Cuffe by Thomas Pole. (Public Domain / Courtesy of New Bedford Whaling Museum)

On April 19, 1812, President James Madison's Non-Intercourse Act prohibiting trade with Great Britain hit mariner and businessman Paul Cuffe hard. On a trip back to the United States from Sierra Leone in West Africa, Cuffe's ship the *Traveller* was confiscated by Newport customs agents when it was found to have both African and British goods aboard.

Cuffe wasted no time taking action to try to reclaim his vessel and its cargo. He secured some letters of support from noted Federalists, and in May traveled to Washington, DC. He hoped to take his claim as high up the governmental chain as was possible—directly to President Madison himself.

On May 2, 1812, Cuffe was at the White House. He met with Secretary of the Treasury Albert Gallatin and then directly with the president. With Madison, he discovered someone who not only was willing to listen to his complaint about his ship being confiscated, but also someone intensely interested in Cuffe's ideas about relocating willing free Black residents to Sierra Leone.

Cuffe was said to address the president by his first name only in that meeting. "James, I have been put to much trouble and have been abused," he told Madison, according to information from the White House Historical Association. "I have come here for thy protections and have to ask thee to order thy collector for the port of Norfolk to clear me out for New Bedford, Massachusetts."

Madison understood Cuffe's use of his first name was not a sign of disrespect, but rather because of Cuffe's Quaker religion. Quakers do not use titles and honorifics when addressing others.

Cuffe's Back-to-Africa initiative would later run head-on into the controversial concept of colonization that would be supported by Madison and many other slave owners. The fact that Cuffe had such a meeting at all with the president is remarkable. Cuffe is believed to be the first free person of color to have a meeting with a president at the White House. In addition, the *Traveller* with its cargo was returned to him.

Paul Cuffe's White House meeting is a standout achievement, but far from his only remarkable feat. A successful mariner and businessman,

Cuffe also was a philanthropist who spoke out for equal treatment of people of color in America. He was likely the wealthiest man of color in the country during part of his lifetime.

Cuffe was born in 1759 on Cuttyhunk Island off the southern coast of Massachusetts. His mother was a member of the Wampanoag tribe. His father, whose name was Kofi Slocum, was a freed slave whose origins were in the modern-day country of Ghana, in Africa. At a young age, Cuffe stopped using the last name Slocum and instead somewhat Anglicized his father's first name to use as his last name.

When Cuffe was about eight years old, his family moved to a 120-acre farm in Dartmouth, Massachusetts. In 1772, Cuffe's father died, leaving the farm to Paul and his brother John. But Cuffe quickly concluded that farming would never be financially lucrative, and he instead turned to a life at sea, as did so many young men of the era who lived in coastal New England communities. While a career as a mariner was hardly without risks and dangers, Cuffe likely also understood it was among the professions where men of color would be respected for the skills they possessed and not confined to specific lowly roles because of the color of their skin.

At the age of just fourteen, Cuffe became a crew member aboard a whaling ship. He learned navigation and also taught himself to read and write. After whaling and trading voyages to the West Indies, Cuffe began his own maritime business. He sailed trading voyages all along the Atlantic coast of America, and also built and owned his own vessels. In 1776, he was taken prisoner by the British and held in a jail in New York for three months. Following his release, he followed a path taken by many New England mariners during the American Revolution and became a privateer, repeatedly eluding the British blockade of the Massachusetts coast to bring provisions to residents on the island of Nantucket.

Cuffe also was keenly aware of racial inequalities in the country and was not afraid to speak out against them. In 1780, he, his brother, and a small group of other Black men petitioned the state of Massachusetts, asking for exemption from taxes for free Blacks and those of mixed-race backgrounds. Cuffe's justification for the request was that he and others of his race were not allowed to vote, and so should not be made to pay taxes.

The petition read, in part: "The petition of several poor negroes and mulattoes, who are inhabitants of the town of Dartmouth, humbly showeth,—That we, being chiefly of the African extract, and by reason of long bondage and hard slavery, have been deprived of enjoying the profits of our labor or the advantage of inheriting estates from our parents, as our neighbors the white people do, having some of us not long enjoyed our own freedom; yet of late, contrary to the invariable custom and practice of the country, we have been, and now are, taxed both in our polls and that small pittance of estate which, through much hard labor and industry, we have got together to sustain ourselves and families."

Cuffe was jailed for nonpayment of taxes, but did succeed in getting his tax burden reduced. The petition also set the stage for major voting reform adopted with the Massachusetts constitution that afforded voting rights to all free men, regardless of racial background.

In 1783, Cuffe married a Native American woman named Alice Abel Pequit. She was a member of the Wampanoag tribe, as had been Cuffe's mother. The couple would have seven children.

By the 1790s, with a wharf and boatyard on what is now called the Westport River, Cuffe began to use some of the wealth he had earned to give back to the community. He gave money to build a Quaker meetinghouse and an integrated public school in Westport, for example. He also wanted to use some of his wealth to directly help free Blacks move to Sierra Leone in Africa, if they wanted to do so.

While some colonizationists saw relocating free Blacks to Africa as a way to remove the threat they posed to the institution of slavery, and others in the group saw it as a means of avoiding having to face a racially integrated society should slavery be abolished, Cuffe's mission was different. He understood only too well the societal obstacles people of color faced in the United States, and believed they could more fully thrive financially and as a community in Africa.

In 1811, Cuffe founded the Friendly Society of Sierra Leone. It was intended to encourage Black settlers there, along with native Africans, to work to establish a prosperous community based on business and trade. In the United States, he established the African Institution with branches in cities such as Baltimore, Philadelphia, Boston, and New

York. The purpose of the Black-run organization was to muster support for Black resettlement.

In December 1815, Cuffe sailed with thirty-eight people of color to resettle in Sierra Leone. Using his ship the *Traveller*, he took the group, whose members ranged from infants to age sixty, to their new home in Africa. It was the first group of Blacks who willingly resettled in Africa from the United States. Cuffe spent $5,000 of his own money (worth more than $100,000 today) to finance the voyage.

Although Cuffe planned for many more voyages to take new settlers to Africa, controversy over the establishment of the American Colonization Society in 1816 led to Cuffe's plans falling out of favor with American Blacks. In January 1817, some three thousand free Black men met at Bethel Church in Philadelphia. They discussed a proposal from the Colonization Society and ultimately renounced any plan to resettle Blacks in Africa.

Their statement read, in part, "Resolved, That we view with deep abhorrence the unmerited stigma attempted to be cast upon the reputation of the free people of color, by the promoters of this measure, 'that they are a dangerous and useless part of the community,' when in the state of disenfranchisement in which we live, in the hour of danger they ceased to remember their wrongs, and rallied around the standard of their country. Resolved, That we never will separate ourselves voluntarily from the slave population in this country; they are our brethren."

Not only was Cuffe seeing his dream of a thriving Black-run African colony wither and die, but he was also now facing serious health problems himself.

Cuffe died on September 7, 1817, and was buried in Westport. Not quite a century after his death, in 1913 a monument honoring Cuffe was dedicated on the grounds of the Quaker meetinghouse in Westport. The monument was given by his great-grandson. The inscription reads, "In Memory of Captain Paul Cuffee. Patriot, Navigator, Educator, Philanthropist, Friend. A Noble Character."

Charlotte Forten Grimké
Writer and Keen Observer of Racial Tensions in Salem

On June 4, 1854, Charlotte Forten recorded in her journal divergent feelings about her adoptive home in Massachusetts, where she had recently moved from Philadelphia.

"A beautiful day. The sky is cloudless, the sun shines warm and bright, and a delicious breeze fans my cheek as I sit by the window writing," the entry began. "How strange it is that in a world so beautiful, there can be so much wickedness; on this delightful day, while many are enjoying themselves in their happy homes, not poor Burns only, but millions beside are suffering in chains; and how many Christian ministers to-day will mention him, or those who suffer with him?"

Forten was just sixteen years old when she wrote these words. She was sent to Salem, Massachusetts, by her wealthy family in 1853 so she could finish her education in integrated schools, which did not exist at the time in Philadelphia. Despite being allowed to attend school with her white peers, first at the Higginson Grammar School, and then, at Salem Normal School (now Salem State University), Forten found Massachusetts to be as full of racial contradictions as was her home city.

Salem, for example, had an active abolitionist movement, a good-sized Black community that included many professionals and highly educated members, and a growing anti-slavery sentiment. Nearby Boston had one of the largest Black communities in the country and was known as a center for abolitionism.

At the same time, even many abolitionists did not believe Blacks had the same intellectual abilities as whites and shunned interracial social fraternization. Even many who fought to end slavery believed in colonization, the movement that sought to resettle American Blacks in Africa.

The Burns that Forten wrote about in June 1854 was Anthony Burns, a man who escaped slavery in Virginia and made his way to Boston. Under the 1850 Fugitive Slave Act that stipulated escaped slaves should be returned to their owners, even if they had made their way to free states, Burns was tried and forced to return south. Many anti-slavery reformers turned out to support him at his trial, but their protests were for naught, although they would later succeed in freeing him.

Forten's journals fill five volumes and chronicle her daily life, along with her political views and innermost thoughts as she finished her education and began a teaching career in Salem. She would go on to teach freed slaves and Black soldiers during the Civil War on the Sea Islands of South Carolina. Her eloquent prose often focuses on the beauty and serenity of the New England seaside landscape north of Boston and typical teen and young adult activities such as sleigh rides and walks by the sea.

Just as frequently, however, she writes about attending anti-slavery lectures, the racism that permeated the society in which she lived, her fervent desire for an end to slavery, and her indignation over the unequal and insulting treatment of members of her race. She often writes about feeling isolated and outcast, longing as only a teenager can to be part of the in-crowd, while also demonstrating a seriousness of purpose far beyond her years. She often seems in despair that slavery persists and that so many of her peers seem unmoved by its injustices. On numerous occasions, most notably around the Fourth of July holiday, she notes in her journals that as long as slavery exists, the United States makes a mockery of its supposed dedication to freedom.

Just three months after her June 1854 entry, and a month after her seventeenth birthday, Forten writes in disgust about friends who were denied entry to a local museum. "Mrs. P [Putnam] and her daughters were refused admission to the Museum, after having tickets given to them, solely on account of their complexion. Insulting language was used to them," she wrote. "I will not attempt to write more. No words can express my feelings. But these cruel wrongs cannot be much longer endured. A day of retribution must come. God grant that it may come very soon!"

An exhibit at Salem's Peabody Essex Museum notes that the East India Marine Society operated a local museum filled with artifacts and interesting objects from around the globe, brought back to Salem by mariners. It barred people of African descent from entering the museum between 1833 and 1865.

On July 13, 1854, Forten wrote in her journal: "I want to go far from my native land where I am hated and oppressed because God has given me a dark skin. How did this cruel, this absurd prejudice ever exist? When I think of it a feeling of indignation rises in my soul too deep for utterance.... When, Oh! Will these dark clouds ever clear away? When will the glorious light of Liberty and Justice appear? The prospect seems very gloomy. But I will try not to despond."

On May 1, 1855, Forten again wrote about her mixed feelings about Salem: "More and more pleasant becomes my Normal School life. Yet, I have made but very few acquaintances and cannot but feel that among all my school companions there is not a single one who gives me her full and entire sympathy. My studies are my truest friends."

A few months later, on September 12, 1855, she wrote again about feeling shunned due to her race:

> *There is one young girl and only one, Miss [Sarah] B[rown], who I believe thoroughly and heartily appreciates anti-slavery—radical anti-slavery—and has no prejudice against color. I wonder that every colored person is not a misanthrope. Surely we have everything to make us hate mankind. I have met girls in the schoolroom—they have been thoroughly kind and cordial to me,—perhaps the next day met them in the street—they feared to recognize me; these I can but regard now with scorn and contempt—once I liked them, believing them incapable of such meanness. Others give the most distant recognition possible. I, of course, acknowledge no such recognitions, and they soon cease entirely.*
>
> *These are but trifles, certainly, to the great, public wrongs that we as a people are obliged to endure. But to those that experience them, these apparent trifles are most wearing and discouraging; even to the child's mind they reveal volumes of deceit and heartlessness, and early*

teach a lesson of suspicion and distrust. Oh! It is hard to go through life meeting contempt with contempt, hatred with hatred, fearing, with too good reason, to love and trust hardly anyone whose skin is white.

Charlotte Forten was born on August 17, 1837, and spent her childhood immersed in a community of activists and abolitionists. According to a short biography of Forten on the Salem State University website, her grandfather James was a Revolutionary War veteran, a successful sailmaker, and one of the most prominent Black abolitionists in the country. The family home frequently hosted the top anti-slavery reformers and speakers of the era. He was a member of the fourth generation of a Philadelphia family of African descent.

The Forten family used some of its wealth to finance slaves buying their freedom and to establish free private schools for Black children. Her father, grandfather, and uncle served on a committee that wrote an 1838 pamphlet titled "An Appeal on Behalf of Forty Thousand Disenfranchised African-Americans." It protested the proposed Pennsylvania constitution that would refuse voting rights to Blacks. The plea was unsuccessful.

When her grandfather James died, his March 11, 1842, funeral procession was "one of the largest funeral processions we ever saw, numbering from three to five thousand persons, white and colored," according to an article in *The Liberator* included in an exhibit in the Charlotte Forten Legacy Room at Salem State University.

Joanne Pope Melish, professor emeritus of history at the University of Kentucky, delivered a lecture about Forten at Salem State University. According to Melish, despite the Forten family's financially comfortable position in Philadelphia, the Fortens were also familiar with white hostility. Although Pennsylvania passed a gradual emancipation law fairly early, in 1780, white mobs repeatedly plundered the neighborhood where the Fortens lived. In 1838, another angry white mob burned down Pennsylvania Hall, the location of a female anti-slavery convention.

Forten's mother died when Charlotte was only three. Her early education was carried out at home, as Philadelphia's schools would not admit Black students. As a teenager, she was sent to Salem by her father to live with the Charles Remond family, noted anti-slavery activists and women's suffrage lecturers, so she could complete her schooling in Massachusetts. She developed close bonds with the Remond family.

Charlotte Forten became the first Black graduate of Salem Normal School and the first Black teacher in Salem. She was a member of the Salem Female Anti-Slavery Society and a founding member of the Philadelphia Female Anti-Slavery Society. She worked as a teacher in Salem, the Sea Islands of South Carolina, and in Washington, DC.

Forten is best known for her writing. Although she repeatedly denigrates the quality of her writing in her journals, editors recognized her talent. She had several anti-slavery poems published, along with essays, letters to the editor, and travel writing. Her work was published by William Lloyd Garrison's *The Liberator*, along with the *Salem Register*, beginning when she was still a student. An essay titled "Glimpses of New England" was published by the *National Anti-Slavery Standard* on June 18, 1858, and a two-part essay describing her experiences teaching on the South Carolina Sea Islands was published in *The Atlantic Monthly*. She developed a strong friendship with the poet John Greenleaf Whittier, who mentored her and encouraged her writing.

Bouts of illness she refers to in her journals as "lung fever"—a term in nineteenth-century parlance that might have referred to tuberculosis—frequently sidelined her teaching career. Still, at the urging of Whittier in 1862, she set out for St. Helena Island in South Carolina, a grueling sea journey. While the Civil War raged not far away, she and a small group of other teachers worked to educate the newly freed slaves and Black soldiers fighting for the Union Army as the 1st South Carolina Volunteers.

On Tuesday night, October 28, 1862, as she arrived in South Carolina, she wrote in her journal: "'Twas a very strange sight as our boat approached the landing at Hilton Head. On the wharf was a motley assemblage—soldiers, officers and 'contrabands' of every hue and size. They were mostly black, however, and certainly the most dismal specimens I ever saw."

The following day, on October 29, she wrote: "We went into the school, and heard the children read and spell. The teachers tell us that they have made great improvement in a very short time, and I noticed with pleasure how bright, how eager to learn many of them seem."

While Forten's journal entries from this time are resplendent with descriptions of the flora of the Sea Islands, she also writes of the challenges of managing large and sometimes unruly groups of students, and the sadness she felt at seeing the poor living conditions and desperate poverty of the local Black community. With an astuteness that seems far ahead of her era, she notes in one entry that she felt it important her students know about some of the great figures of Black history. As such, she taught them about Toussaint L'Ouverture, a former slave who became a leader of the Haitian Revolution that established the world's first Black republic.

After the Civil War, despite continued bouts of serious illness, Forten moved in 1872 to Washington, DC, where she taught at the Preparatory High School for Negro Youth, according to information in the exhibit at Salem State University. At the time, it was the only college-preparatory high school for Blacks in the nation's capital city. The school was housed in the Fifteenth Street Presbyterian Church. Forten left her teaching position there after just a year and took a job with the US Treasury Department.

In 1878, she married Reverend Francis Grimké, pastor of Fifteenth Street Presbyterian Church. She had already passed her fortieth birthday by this time. Her husband was the son of an enslaved woman and a South Carolina planter. The Grimkés had just one child, a daughter they named Theodora Cornelia, who died at only six months old.

Charlotte Forten Grimké died on July 23, 1914, in Washington, DC. Some twenty-two years earlier, in 1892, she made her final journal entry, ending more than five decades of chronicling both the everyday and the extraordinary events of her lifetime. Despite her family's wealth, her genteel upbringing, her advanced education, her notable professional career, and her writing talents, her journals demonstrate how no Black citizen of that time period could escape the ever-present racial prejudice and repeated insults of a society that viewed Blacks as inferior.

Charlotte Forten and her remarkable accomplishments as an abolitionist and women's rights activist are recognized by her alma mater, which is now Salem State University. In 2019, Salem also developed a 25,000-square-foot waterfront park and named it in her honor.

Charlotte Forten Grimké and child. (Library Company of Philadelphia / Annie Webb Papers Collection)

Prince Hall
Pioneer in Black Masonry

Prince Hall was a man ahead of his time. He was one of the first people of color to use the wording in the Declaration of Independence to make a case for freedom and civil rights for Blacks; among the first to advocate for high-quality education for children of color; was a very early supporter of the Back-to-Africa Movement; and was the first to establish an African Lodge of the Free and Accepted Masons.

A portrait depicting what Prince Hall may have looked like. (Public Domain / Courtesy of Wikimedia Commons and Grand Lodge of British Columbia and Yukon)

While these accomplishments earn Hall a place of prominence among Black American activists, what is perhaps most notable is *when* he achieved these milestones. It was years—in some cases, decades—before the abolitionist movement had blossomed or there was much advocacy for Black civil rights.

In January 1777, for example, Hall wrote and submitted a petition to the Massachusetts legislature asking for the initiation of the process of gradual emancipation of slaves. The petition, also signed by other free Blacks, was submitted just months after the Declaration of Independence was signed by white patriots.

The Atlantic included an excerpt from the petition in a March 2021 article (retaining original spelling and style):

> *The petition of A Great Number of Blackes detained in a State of Slavery in the Bowels of a free & Christian Country Humbly shuwith that your Petitioners Apprehend that Thay have in Common with all other men a Natural and Unaliable Right to that freedom which the Grat—Parent of the Unavese hath Bestowed equalley on all menkind and which they have Never forfuted by Any Compact or Agreement whatever—but thay wher Unjustly Dragged by the hand of cruel Power from their Derest frinds and sum of them Even torn from the Embraces of their tender Parents—from A popolous Plasant And plentiful cuntry And in Violation of Laws of Nature and off Nations And in defiance of all the tender feelings of humanity Brough hear Either to Be sold Like Beast of Burthen & Like them Condemnd to Slavery for Life.*

The petition was unsuccessful. Massachusetts abolished slavery in 1783, based on legal interpretations of its 1780 constitution.

Accounts of Prince Hall's early life are somewhat murky. Different sources include various pieces of information that are not agreed upon by all scholars. Some sources say he was born free, while others state that he started life as an enslaved person. Some say he was born in Barbados and others that he was born in Boston. Some sources say he was married several times while others are less certain about his possible marriages.

(Apparently there were several men named Prince Hall who lived at about the same time period and in the same geographic location, which may explain some of the conflicts among sources.)

What does seem certain is that this Prince Hall was born around 1735. Again, while there is disagreement about the place of his birth and his status as a free or enslaved person, it is agreed that he was a leatherworker in Boston in the years before the American Revolution. He served in the Revolution and urged other Blacks to do the same, and in the years immediately following the war, he became one of the most prominent members of, and spokesman for, Boston's free Black community.

The Medford Historical Society, located in the town just outside Boston where Hall lived for a time, contends that he arrived in Boston when he was about seventeen years old. He settled in Medford and was married, but his new wife died shortly after their wedding. In 1756, he had a son named Primus with a woman named Delia. He may or may not have been married to her. By the time he was twenty-five, an article by the Society states that Hall owned real estate and was eligible to vote. He fought with the Continental troops at the Battle of Bunker Hill.

Even before the war, he was already making himself known to Massachusetts officials. In 1773, for example, he petitioned the colony's senate to provide the means for free Blacks—who chose to do so—to emigrate to Africa.

One of Hall's most significant accomplishments was the establishment of the first Masonic Lodge for Blacks in America. While today the mysterious fraternal organization doesn't hold quite the prestige or societal sway it once did, the command of Masonry in colonial America shouldn't be underestimated. Powerful and influential men such as George Washington were Masons.

In 1775, Hall and fourteen other free Blacks became members of the British Army Lodge No. 441. When the British left Boston, Hall and the other free Blacks formed their own lodge, one that became the independent African Lodge No. 1. Not only was Freemasonry viewed as a pathway to respect and honor in the larger community, but Hall's lodge also operated as a mutual aid society for the Black community. The organization provided community strength and mutual support at a time when Blacks frequently struggled with financial hardships and almost daily felt the impacts of ubiquitous racial prejudice.

The Masons supported those who needed a variety of types of assistance in a time when there were few other options for those who became ill or lost jobs. The Black Masons ran food drives, brought free firewood to those who needed it, and provided weekly stipends to the unemployed. Between 1775 and 1784, more than fifty Black men participated in the lodge.

Hall also used his position as the so-called Worshipful Master of the Black Masons to speak out on issues of importance to the community, including civil rights, the abolition of slavery, and educational opportunities. It is believed that Hall had a hand in assisting a formerly enslaved woman named Belinda Royall in petitioning the Massachusetts General Court in 1783 for a pension from the estate of her enslaver. Royall eventually was successful in her efforts. This case is cited as the first example of reparations granted for slavery.

In October 1787, Hall and others petitioned the Massachusetts legislature, asking that schools for Black children be established. When that and subsequent petitions were unsuccessful, Hall started a school for Black children in his own home.

In 1788, another petition spoke against the treatment of specific individuals who were free Blacks. They had been kidnapped and sold into slavery, and Hall asked for their return. One of the men was successful in securing his emancipation because of his involvement with the Masons. When he was being offered for sale as a slave, it was discovered that the man who was buying him also was a Mason. Because of this common bond, the Black man was freed.

In June 1797, Hall's final published speech to his fellow Masons spoke of the daily injustices suffered by Boston's Black community. In part of the speech, he said: "Patience, I say; for were we not possessed of a great measure of it, we could not bear up under the daily insults we meet with in the streets of Boston, much more on public days of recreation. How, at such times, are we shamefully abused, and that to such a degree, that we may truly be said to carry our lives in our hands, and the arrows of death are flying about our heads. . . . 'Tis not for want of courage in you, for they know that they dare not face you man for man, but in a mob, which we despise."

Prince Hall died in 1807, well before the cause of abolition and Black civil rights began to expand. He was buried in Copp's Hill Burying Ground in Boston, in the Masonic tradition. The year after his death, the Masonic lodge he founded was renamed in his honor as the Prince Hall Masons. It became the most influential Black fraternal organization in the 1800s, and remains a strong organization, with more than 300,000 Prince Hall Masons today. Even so, in the state Hall called home for most of his life, racial prejudice led the Grand Masonic Lodge of Massachusetts to shun formal recognition of the Prince Hall Masons until after the Civil War.

Prince Hall Memorial Day ceremony at Prince Hall Cemetery, Arlington, Massachusetts, May 2002. (Courtesy of Arlington Historical Society)

Lewis Hayden
Self-Emancipated Slave Elected as Massachusetts Official

Portrait of Lewis Hayden. (Courtesy of League of Women for Community Service)

Lewis Hayden

When Lewis Hayden died on April 7, 1889, the *New York Times* ran a front-page obituary that included this sentiment: "Lewis Hayden, who died to-day, was one of the most widely known and highly respected colored citizens of [Boston]. His life was notable as including active participation in many of the events, local and national, connected with the agitation for the abolition of slavery."

The *Daily Inter Ocean* of Chicago reported on April 12, 1889, about Hayden's funeral, writing, "Probably no colored man who has passed away in Boston has been honored with a more imposing demonstration, or greater evidence of esteem, than took place to-day in connection with the funeral of Mr. Lewis Hayden."

On the day of his funeral, a procession of hundreds made its way from Hayden's home in the Beacon Hill neighborhood of Boston to the African Methodist Episcopal Church, where the ceremony was conducted. The church was filled to its capacity of 1,200. The Boston Common Council issued a proclamation after Hayden's death that read, in part, "One of the pioneers in the freeing of this country from the curse of slavery; the City of Boston has lost an honorable and upright man and a consistent friend of humanity."

These widespread adulations are not surprising given Hayden's life story. In a community of Black reformers and abolitionists whose achievements were many, Hayden's accomplishments put him at the pinnacle of that amazing group of courageous citizens.

Born into slavery in Kentucky, Hayden knew firsthand the heartbreak of family separation and the dehumanization and brutality of the institution. He and his wife and son escaped from slavery, taking the dangerous journey north to Canada before eventually finding their way to the large Black community in Boston. In Boston, the self-educated Hayden became a leader in abolition efforts, a foremost conductor on the Underground Railroad, a businessman who ran a clothing store, and, ultimately, an elected member of the Massachusetts legislature. The *New York Times* obituary also noted that Hayden "made several contributions to Masonic literature, was active in his efforts on behalf of equal school privileges for white and colored children, and was an advocate of temperance and woman suffrage."

Hayden was born in Lexington, Kentucky, around 1811. His mother and father suffered the heartbreak of being ripped apart from each other when his father's owner moved and took his father with him. Hayden recalled that his mother, who was of mixed Native American and white heritage, suffered severe mental trauma because of these barbaric practices of slavery. At one point, he said that she appeared ready to kill Hayden rather than see him continue his life in slavery, a scenario that author Harriet Beecher Stowe used as inspiration for inclusion in her seminal abolitionist novel, *Uncle Tom's Cabin*.

Hayden also saw his siblings sold off by the Presbyterian minister Adam Rankin, who owned the family. Hayden recalled later, "When he [Rankin] was going to leave Kentucky for Pennsylvania, he sold all my brothers and sisters at auction. I stood by and saw them sold. When I was just going up on the block, he swapped me off for a pair of carriage horses." Hayden said he was told that in church, Rankin frequently preached that there was no more harm in separating families of enslaved workers than there was in separating a litter of piglets.

Hayden suffered also at the hands of Henry Clay, the Kentucky lawyer and longtime politician who served in both the US Senate and the House of Representatives. Hayden's first wife and two children were owned by Clay, who had a complicated relationship with the institution of slavery. Although a lifelong slaveholder himself, Clay advocated for the gradual emancipation of slaves in Kentucky, and also joined a group of those who pushed for colonization.

One of Hayden's first two children died, but Clay sold Hayden's other child, along with Hayden's wife. Hayden would never see them again, and later wrote about the traumatic incident: "I have one child who is buried in Kentucky and that grave is pleasant to think of. I've got another that is sold nobody knows where, and that I can never bear to think of."

After Hayden remarried and was leased by his owner to work as a waiter at Lexington's Phoenix Hotel, he met a Northern white couple who spoke to him about escaping from slavery. Soon, Hayden, his wife Harriet, and son Joseph, aided by the abolitionist couple, made their escape. The couple, Calvin Fairbank and Delia Webster, were caught by officials and punished for their role in the Hayden family's escape. Webster was sentenced to two years of hard labor and Fairbank to fifteen years in prison.

The Haydens, however, were successful in escaping slavery. They made the treacherous journey all the way to Canada, but later returned to the United States—first to Detroit, then New Bedford, Massachusetts, and, finally, in 1846, to Boston.

The couple quickly became involved in the community of Black reformers and activists living in Boston's Beacon Hill neighborhood. Harriet Hayden began operating a boardinghouse out of their home, and Hayden established a men's clothing store on Cambridge Street. Both the home and store served as centers of anti-slavery activities, and the Haydens assisted more than one hundred escaping slaves en route north on the Underground Railroad. The Hayden home became known as the "Temple of Refuge."

After the passage of the Fugitive Slave Act of 1850, a law that required the return of escaped slaves to their owners even if those slaves had reached free states, Hayden became active in the vigilance committee dedicated to assisting and sheltering these refugees from being forced back into slavery. In 1850, the Haydens sheltered William and Ellen Craft, a couple who had escaped slavery in Georgia. Hayden apparently made it known that he kept a store of gunpowder in the house and was willing to blow up the building rather than turn over to slave catchers any self-emancipated slave in his care.

William Lloyd Garrison's abolitionist newspaper *The Liberator*, according to an article on the National Park Service website, reported that a US marshal pursuing the Crafts called off the arrest because "He knew that the road to hell lay over Lewis Hayden's threshold; and the cost to him would be rather more than the Slave Power would be ready to make up to him."

Hayden was also a leader in freeing a former slave who was working in Boston and taken into custody under the Fugitive Slave Act, in 1851. Hayden was among a mob that broke into the Suffolk County Courthouse where Shadrach Minkins was being held. Minkins was freed and helped on his way to safety. Hayden was arrested for his part in helping to free Minkins.

Hayden was also part of a group that unsuccessfully tried to free two other formerly enslaved men who were victims of the Fugitive Slave Act. The high-profile cases of Thomas Sims and Anthony Burns ended with those men being returned to slavery in the South.

In 1858, Hayden became a messenger to the Massachusetts Secretary of State's office, a position he held until nearly the end of his life. It's believed he was the first Black employee of the Massachusetts Commonwealth.

During the Civil War, Hayden recruited men to serve in the famous Massachusetts 54th Regiment. The regiment was formed in 1863, organized by Hayden's friend, Governor John A. Andrew. Recruitment efforts were successful enough that a second Black Massachusetts regiment also was formed. The 54th demonstrated the battle-readiness of Black soldiers when they participated in the assault on Battery Wagner, a strategic post guarding the harbor of Charleston, South Carolina. Union troops were defeated militarily, and while the 54th suffered 42 percent casualties, the regiment opened the door for many more Black recruits. Some 180,000 Black men ultimately joined the Union's military forces.

Although Hayden enthusiastically supported having Black men fighting for the Union, the war brought him more personal heartbreak. His son Joseph, who was in the Union Navy, died in the war.

After the war, Hayden was elected to the Massachusetts General Court, the commonwealth's legislature. While there, he advocated for women's rights, including voting rights. He also was a leader in the effort to erect a memorial to Crispus Attucks, a man of color who was killed at the 1770 Boston Massacre. The memorial was unveiled on Boston Common in 1888, after which Hayden was said to remark, "I am happy and ready to die now. They cannot take from us this record of history showing that we participated in the revolution to secure American Liberty, as we have participated in every great movement in the best interests of the country since."

Indeed, it was not long after this that Hayden died of kidney disease. His widow Harriet lived until 1893. She had one more gift to give to the people of color in the Boston community. Harriet left her estate, valued at about $5,000, to provide scholarships to Harvard Medical School for needy students of color. The Lewis and Harriet Hayden Scholarship for Colored Students remains in place today.

William Cooper Nell
Pioneering Black Historian Who Fought for Integrated Education

William Cooper Nell. (Collection of the Massachusetts Historical Society)

Feeling the personal sting of racism at an early age helped set William Cooper Nell on a path toward activism and community organizing, to advocate for equal rights for people of color. As a boy, he attended classes at the Abiel Smith School for Black children that operated out of the basement of the African Meeting House, located near Nell's Beacon Hill home. When he was twelve years old, Nell's outstanding academic achievements were recognized with the Franklin Medal, an award presented to children who scored exceptionally well on a citywide exam.

Despite being a top scholar in Boston, Nell and two of his classmates were not allowed to receive the award at a dinner ceremony at Faneuil Hall because of their race. Determined to attend the event anyway, Nell got himself hired as a waiter for the evening. As such, he could view the ceremony only as an outsider rather than a participant, and was denied the deserved public acknowledgment of his academic achievement. Nell later said the incident led him to make a promise: "God willing, I will do my best to hasten the day when the color of the skin will be no barrier to equal school rights." Nell became an ardent organizer for integrated schools that would offer equal education to all students.

While this event provided Nell with one more reason to dedicate his life to equal rights activism, the foundation for such activities was laid from the time of his birth. Nell was born in December 1816, and grew up in the free Black community on the northern slope of Beacon Hill in Boston. He was surrounded by reformers and abolitionists whose thoughts and actions were considered radical at the time. His parents, William Guion Nell and Louisa Marshall, were among these forward-thinking residents.

Nell's father's roots were in the free Black community of Charleston, South Carolina. His mother was from Brookline, just outside of Boston. Both were Black activists in the Boston community. In 1826, his father helped found the Massachusetts General Colored Association that was dedicated to ending slavery and racial discrimination. He petitioned to end slavery in the country and advocated for an end to laws that discriminated against members of the Black community. Nell's mother joined the Boston Female Anti-Slavery Society.

Nell was enthralled by the activism he witnessed around him in one of New England's largest Black communities. In January 1832, he stood outside in a snowstorm watching a group of men that included noted abolitionist William Lloyd Garrison as they established an anti-slavery organization. According to an article on the National Park Service website, Nell later recalled the event in this manner: "I remember, when a boy, in January 1832, looking in at the vestry window off of Belknap Street Church, while the editor of *The Liberator* and a faithful few organized the first Anti-Slavery Society."

Nell himself became a faithful adherent of Garrison's radical abolitionism. When he was still a teenager, Nell helped form an abolitionist youth organization called the Juvenile Garrison Independent Society. He spoke to the society in October 1833, when he was just sixteen years old. In the speech, Nell declared, in part: "Prejudice is the cause of slavery, and its attendant evils; and which, united with malice, is the cause of disunion in societies, and is the fomenter of all commotion."

Nell also fervently believed, as did Garrison, in the racial integration of organizations and institutions. This belief put Nell at odds with members of his own community when he fought for years to close the Abiel Smith School, instead advocating for a completely integrated public school system in the city of Boston. The African School was established by members of the Black community in 1798, and many members of the community supported it throughout Nell's fight for school integration.

Nell persisted, however. His struggle lasted for nearly fifteen years and included protests, petitions, and boycotts. Nell also helped found the School Abolishing Party. In 1855, moved by Nell's and his supporters' efforts, the legislature integrated the public schools. The Black community honored Nell's long fight for school integration at a December 17, 1855, event called a "Triumph of Equal School Rights."

Dorothy Porter Wesley, a Howard University librarian and bibliographer who studied and wrote about Nell, wrote that after the successful campaign for school integration, Nell recalled seeing a Black child walking by the Abiel Smith School and saying, "Good-bye forever, colored school. Tomorrow we are like the other Boston boys." Nell no doubt found great satisfaction in hearing this exclamation that validated his efforts.

Nell also understood and effectively used the power of the pen. He began working for Garrison as an office boy at *The Liberator* when he was still a teenager. Nell contributed writings for nearly all of the thirty-five years it was published weekly, and served in myriad roles at the publication. Nell also accompanied Garrison on some of his lecture tours and addressed the audiences along with the white Garrison.

Nell broke with Garrison for just a few years in the 1840s, when he went to work for famed Black abolitionist Frederick Douglass in Rochester, New York, where Douglass had started publishing his own abolitionist newspaper, called *The North Star*. Nell soon returned to Boston and *The Liberator*, however.

Besides his journalism, Nell is renowned as the first Black historian. His 1855 book *The Colored Patriots of the American Revolution* honors the contributions of Black Americans in military service, with profiles of heroes such as Crispus Attucks, who was killed in the 1770 Boston Massacre. Nell's book includes an introduction by Harriet Beecher Stowe, famed author of *Uncle Tom's Cabin*.

According to a National Park Service article, in the conclusion of the volume, Nell wrote: "If others fail to appreciate the merit of the colored man, let us cherish the deserted shrine. The names which others reject should only be the more sacredly [in] our care. Let us keep them for the hoped-for day of full emancipation, when, in the possession of all our rights, and redeemed from the long night of ignorance that has rested over us, we may recall them to memory."

Besides speaking and writing about the need to abolish slavery and extend civil rights to people of color, Nell was active in the Underground Railroad, harboring escaped slaves when he could. In Boston in 1854, Nell led efforts to free a man named Anthony Burns, who had escaped enslavement in Virginia but was arrested and tried in Boston and returned to slavery. A group of Black residents forcibly entered the courthouse where Burns was being held, but were unsuccessful in freeing him. Eventually, Boston abolitionists did buy Burns his freedom, and he went on to be educated at Oberlin College. The Burns case was also the last time the Fugitive Slave Act was enforced in Massachusetts.

The country's fight over slavery was coming to a head as the United States marched ever closer to the Civil War. In 1861, Nell achieved another first among people of color when he became the first Black civil servant, nominated for a position as clerk in the post office.

Nell lived to see an end to slavery in the United States, a vindication of much of his life's work. Sadly, he was only fifty-seven years old when he died of a stroke in May 1874, less than a decade after the close of the bloody Civil War. William Lloyd Garrison delivered a eulogy at Nell's funeral before Nell was buried in Forest Hills Cemetery in Jamaica Plain. Garrison himself would be buried in the same cemetery when he died five years later.

Despite his life's accomplishments, Nell's grave remained unmarked until 1989, when Dorothy Porter Wesley and a group of community activists from Nell's home city finally erected a monument marking the burial place of this great American hero.

Sarah Parker Remond
Left America in Search of Racial Acceptance

Sarah Parker Remond was born in Salem, Massachusetts, into an activist family accustomed to advocating for their rights and those of other people of color. She gave her first anti-slavery lecture when she was just sixteen years old and sometimes toured with her brother Charles Lenox Remond to speak about abolitionism.

Despite the family's dedication to the causes of abolition and civil rights for Blacks, however, by the time she was forty-one years old, she had apparently given up on the possibility of earning such rights in America for herself. On an application to become a naturalized British citizen, she wrote in September 1865, "The strong prejudice against persons of African descent which is entertained by a large proportion of the Inhabitants of the United States and the social disabilities under which such persons consequently suffer have determined your Memorialist [applicant] under no circumstances to return to reside in America."

It was a sad and stark reminder that despite the recent end of the US Civil War that had finally abolished slavery in the country, and the hope that Reconstruction gave to Blacks in the South, Black Americans still faced racial hatred, harassment, and violence. Sarah Parker Remond had seen and experienced enough in her native country that she had given up hope that daily life would change for people of color in America. She was true to her words on the naturalization application, never returning to live in the United States.

Sarah Parker Remond was born in 1826, at a time when the abolitionist fight was heating up in the Northern states. She was the seventh of eight children, although some sources indicate there were more children in the family. Her parents John and Nancy Lenox Remond were accomplished caterers, well known for the delicious fare they provided for many parties and events in Salem. They also ran a hairdressing business and took in boarders, including Charlotte Forten, who lived with the Remonds while she studied in Salem.

Remond's father had come from Curacao to Massachusetts in 1798 as a free person of color. Her mother was born in Massachusetts and was the daughter of a Revolutionary War veteran. When Remond was a child, her parents sought to enroll her in a private school, but she was not admitted because of her race. She and her sisters were admitted into a local high school, but then expelled because local officials said they were planning a separate school for Black children. Remond later recalled the incident made her feel like Hester Prynne, the Nathaniel Hawthorne character who was forced to be a social outcast because she'd had a child out of wedlock.

In May 1853, Remond and some companions went to Boston's Howard Athenaeum to see a performance of the opera *Don Pasquale*. She was forced to leave because of her race and then pushed down a flight of stairs when she refused to sit in the separate section reserved for Blacks. She filed suit against the agent for the opera troupe and a police officer and won the case. The theater was ordered to integrate, according to information on the Iowa State University website. It was one of the earliest cases challenging segregation in public places.

In November 1853, Remond again found herself and a friend barred from touring a public exhibition at the Franklin Institute in Philadelphia. Charges against a police officer in that incident were dropped, according to the Massachusetts Historical Society.

In the late 1850s, Remond was hired by the American Anti-Slavery Society to tour numerous states to speak about abolition. In 1859, she began her studies at Bedford College in London, because she believed she would not get a solid education in the United States. While there, she continued to present both anti-slavery and women's rights speeches.

Remond earned a reputation as a strident and direct speaker who did not shy away from connecting the textile mills that powered the economy in parts of England to the misery of the enslaved people who toiled in the cotton fields of the American South. Besides pointing out this complicity in perpetuating the system of slavery in the United States, she also addressed the horrors of sexual abuse suffered by enslaved girls and women at the hands of their white owners.

"When I walk through the streets of Manchester and meet load after load of cotton, I think of those eighty thousand cotton plantations on which was grown the one hundred and twenty-five millions of dollars' worth of cotton which supply your market, and I remember that not one cent of the money ever reached the hands of the labourers," she said in an 1859 speech in that city, according to Global Threads, a website focused on telling the history of the cotton industry in Manchester, England.

After a speech she gave in Warrington, a town located between the industrial giants of Manchester and Liverpool, Remond was presented with a silver watch and addressed as a sister to the women there. "I have been received as a sister by white women for the first time in my life," she said, according to Global Threads. "I have received a sympathy I never was offered before."

From 1859 to 1861, Remond continued her studies at Bedford College while keeping up with her anti-slavery activities. She also studied nursing at London University College. In 1866, she was among some 1,500 women, and likely the only Black woman, to sign a petition advocating for women's suffrage in Britain.

In 1862, she addressed the International Congress of Charities, Correction and Philanthropy in London, talking about the state of enslaved people in the United States. At the end of her speech, she said:

> *The real capacities of the negro race have never been thoroughly tested; and until they are placed in a position to be influenced by the civilizing influences which surround freemen, it is really unjust to apply to them the same test, or to expect them to attain the same standard of excellence, as if a fair opportunity had been given to develop their faculties. With all the demoralizing influences by which they are surrounded, they still retain far more of that which is humanizing than their masters. No such acts of cruelty have ever emanated from the victims of slavery in the Southern states as have been again and again practised by their masters.*

Shortly thereafter, Remond moved to Italy. Now in her forties, she became a medical student in Florence. At age fifty, she married an Italian man, and the couple lived in Florence, after which they moved to Rome, where she spent her final years in the practice of medicine. Her life at this point became much more private, but in 1886 Frederick Douglass visited Italy and reported that he saw Remond and two of her sisters living there. She died in 1894 and is buried in Rome.

Sarah Parker Remond. (Collection of the Massachusetts Historical Society)

New Hampshire
A Mixed Record on Abolitionism

The African Burying Ground memorial in Portsmouth. An eighteenth-century African burial ground was paved over, and later rediscovered during a construction project in 2003. The memorial park honors those who were buried, then forgotten. (Author's Collection)

In 1846, poet John Greenleaf Whittier wrote an ode to New Hampshire that praised it for being the first state to send an openly abolitionist senator—John P. Hale of Dover—to Washington, DC. Whittier, an avowed abolitionist, called New Hampshire a brave state for this action.

In terms of its actual record regarding slavery and abolition, New Hampshire was no more or less brave than other states in New England. Slavery existed within its borders, just as it did in other New England states. New Hampshire also never overtly banned slavery. While its 1783 constitution declared "all men are born equal and independent," no judicial records in the state indicate this was construed as ending slavery there.

In addition, the lure of the financial wealth the slave trade could bring called as loudly to New Hampshire mariners as it did to those in other areas. Ship owners in Portsmouth participated in the slave trade and, because New Hampshire did not impose a tariff on slaves, the colony was a base through which slaves were brought to America before being shipped elsewhere. Many New Hampshire ships carried a few slaves along with other cargo to sell. In 1755, a ship called the *Exeter*, owned by John Moffatt, brought sixty-one enslaved men, women, and children to New Hampshire. They likely were sold at various locations along the East Coast.

In the earliest colonial days, most enslaved people in New England were Native Americans, but the number of enslaved people of African descent grew during the eighteenth century. In 1708, 70 Negro slaves were reported as living in or near the New Hampshire coast. In 1775, there were 656 slaves in New Hampshire. Most enslaved people lived in or near Portsmouth.

By the eighteenth century, laws began to be passed, in New Hampshire as in other colonies, that restricted the activities of the enslaved and servants; for example, they could not move about towns without their masters' permission, could not be out after dark, and were not allowed to drink in public taverns.

Christy Clark-Pujara, professor of history and Afro-American studies at the University of Wisconsin–Madison, is quoted in an article, "Slavery Persisted in New England Until the 19th Century" (posted on

History.com) as saying, "There is a strong fiction that slavery was mild in the North. There is absolutely no historical evidence to support that. Bondage was bondage ... people were beaten and tortured in the North, just like they were beaten and tortured in the South, and it was just as bad in different ways."

Still, enslaved men in the North found some reason to be hopeful as the colonies rebelled against England. During the American Revolution, there were 139 Black men who served in New Hampshire's military forces. After the war, in 1779, Prince Whipple, an enslaved man from Portsmouth who had served in the military, joined with 18 other Black men in petitioning New Hampshire's state government. They contended they should be emancipated because of their military service. Their plea was ignored.

By the nineteenth century, with the abolitionist movement growing, New Hampshire's record was somewhat mixed. There were two abolitionist newspapers in the state, but local abolitionist organizations often were mired in political divisions. There was a statewide abolitionist society, but New Hampshire also was the only Eastern state that did not send candidates to a Buffalo abolitionist convention in 1843. Only 126 of an estimated 2,000 abolitionist voters in the state voted in 1840 for the abolitionist Liberty Party's candidate for president.

Early colonizationists in New Hampshire, where the movement was relatively popular, did hold beliefs that mirrored those of later abolitionists. In the 1820s, many advocated for an end to slavery and more equal treatment of people of all races. Stephen Lawrence Cox writes in his 1980 doctoral dissertation for the University of New Hampshire:

> *While the colonizationist indictment of slavery and prejudice laid the foundation for the anti-slavery movement in New Hampshire in the 1820s, many colonizationists were ... being won over to the cause of immediate emancipation by the early 1830s. Several reasons explain the growing dissatisfaction with colonization schemes. First, there had been little success with colonizing efforts. Not only was the death rate high for early settlers in Liberia, but constant attacks by hostile tribes threatened any permanent, stable settlement. Also, the discovery*

that most free blacks shunned emigration seriously undermined colonizationist activity. Finally, and perhaps most disturbing, was the realization that many colonizationists, especially in the South, were not embracing the scheme out of Christian charity; rather, many adherents merely sought to rid the country of free blacks because they were a nuisance and a potential danger.

Racism also was fairly widespread in the state, just as it was in most locations in America up through the nineteenth century. In one particularly stark display, in 1835, a mob protesting the existence of a racially integrated school in Canaan called Noyes Academy succeeded in pulling the school building off its foundation and leaving it in a ruined and crumpled heap.

By the time of the Civil War, some 125 Black men from the state fought to end slavery and preserve the Union. Among these were Aaron and William Hall of Exeter, who joined the famed 54th Massachusetts Infantry Regiment and fought in the Battle of Olustee, near Jacksonville, Florida. A third brother, Moses, enlisted in Company C, 3rd US Colored Infantry. The Hall brothers' grandfather was Jude Hall, a celebrated Black New Hampshire soldier of the Revolution. Despite Jude Hall's battlefield valor, the family lived in poverty after the Revolution, and Jude Hall saw three of his sons sold into slavery because of petty debts.

Slavery in New Hampshire officially ended with the ratification of the Thirteenth Amendment to the Constitution in 1865. While slavery was never as widespread in New Hampshire as it was in some locations in America, it did exist, and was tolerated for many years. And, as in other parts of New England, racism and unequal treatment of Blacks was common.

Julia Williams Garnet
Fighting for an Education

Julia Williams demonstrated incredible determination to secure an education in the early nineteenth century. That determination would be tested by violence and destruction.

Born in Charleston, South Carolina, in 1811, Williams moved with her family to Boston when she was a child. While many sources contend Williams was born free, some say she actually was born into slavery. Regardless of her original status, by the time she was a young woman, she was eager to complete an education. At age twenty-one, she traveled to rural eastern Connecticut, where Prudence Crandall was operating a female academy for young women of color. But at a time when increasing abolitionist sympathy also was unleashing an uptick in pushback by racists who spread fear among their neighbors about an onslaught of Blacks in their midst, Crandall's school enjoyed a very short tenure.

The townspeople in Canterbury, Connecticut, succeeded in driving Crandall out of business through both harassment and violence. The legislature also passed a bill in 1833 that outlawed the education of Blacks from other states within the boundaries of Connecticut without local approval. Williams and other Black scholars whose schooling was cut short in Canterbury then sought other opportunities to complete their education.

Williams headed north to New Hampshire. In the small town of Canaan, located just to the east of Hanover, home to Dartmouth College, four residents who were abolitionists had raised funds to establish a college preparatory school dedicated to educating students of all racial backgrounds. Dartmouth had begun admitting Black students in the early 1800s, and the need for schools that would provide Black students with a pipeline to institutions of higher education was well known.

Acrylic painting depicting the destruction of Noyes Academy in Canaan, by Mikel Wells (1999). (Town of Canaan / New Hampshire Museum)

Noyes Academy, named for Samuel Noyes, the Canaan farmer who first raised money to establish the school, was chartered by the state of New Hampshire in July 1834 and opened the following month. The school was one of a few in that time period that was both racially integrated and coeducational. A history of Noyes Academy on the Canaan, New Hampshire, website notes that most of the locals at first either supported the integrated education to be offered at Noyes Academy, or at least did not overtly oppose it. Forty-nine of the school's incorporators voted in favor of integrated education, while just two voted against it. The students also easily found willing local families with whom to lodge while studying at the academy.

That sentiment quickly shifted, however, once the school opened. Newspaper editorials throughout the state stoked fears about the academy. Editorial writers warned that abolition would bring a flood of Blacks to New England, putting white mill employees out of work. Furthermore, the editorials warned against touching off a civil war of the type that did erupt in America some thirty years later. Finally, one of the most common warnings from the fearmongers was the threat of Black men preying on white women in the community—a common and false racial stereotype used as a weapon of subjugation for decades.

Less than a year after the school was established, the sentiment against it reached its zenith. A mob wielding axes and carrying torches gathered at the school building on July 4, 1835, and threatened to destroy the academy. While a town magistrate who also was a school trustee headed off the violence that day, those against the school took the issue to a town meeting vote.

According to the school history on the Canaan website, while there were only about three hundred voters in town at the time, more than four hundred turned out for the town meeting. Assuming they were protected legally by the town meeting vote against the school, a liquored-up angry mob arrived at the school building on August 10, 1835, armed with teams of oxen and plenty of chains.

In an act even more drastic than the violence perpetrated against Crandall's academy, and no doubt terrifying to the Noyes Academy students, the mob dragged the school from its foundation. Over the course of two days, the building was pulled down the road and deposited in a heap of rubble near the town's meetinghouse.

With another educational dream shattered, Williams and other Noyes Academy students were left once again searching for a school. Williams, along with three other former Noyes Academy students, now headed out of New England to Whitesboro, New York, just outside Utica, to attend classes at Oneida Institute. Oneida Institute was known as a radical school at the forefront of abolitionist thought in the country.

Another Noyes student who went to Oneida was Williams's future husband, Henry Highland Garnet. Following her tumultuous education, Williams went to Boston and became a teacher in a school for young women of color run by Martha and Lucy Ball. She also taught Sunday school and became active in charitable pursuits.

Besides beginning a career, Williams also was becoming an reformer who believed deeply in the importance of better education for people of color. She joined the Boston Female Anti-Slavery Society and was one of four delegates from that group sent to the 1837 Anti-Slavery Convention of American Women in New York. While there, she again crossed paths with Garnet. The two shared some meals and conversations and, judging by his writings, Garnet became smitten with Williams.

Garnet was teaching in a school for Black children in New York City and conducting religious meetings. In 1841, he was ordained in the Presbyterian Church, and he and Julia Williams married. They moved to Troy, New York, in 1842 when Garnet became pastor of the Liberty Street Presbyterian Church. The couple had three children, but only one survived to adulthood.

Williams often counseled Garnet about the speeches and sermons he gave. She participated in preparing the speech he delivered in 1843 at the Annual Convention of the Colored Citizens of New York State in Buffalo. In the fiery speech, he urged the enslaved to rise up and fight for their freedom.

In New York, Williams remained active in abolitionist groups. By 1852, the couple moved to Jamaica, working as missionaries there. Williams Garnet headed a school that trained and prepared young women with little financial means for domestic work.

The couple did not stay in Jamaica for very long, and when they returned to the United States, they went to Washington, DC, where Williams Garnet remained active and found a new and necessary way to help people of color. Although the Union was forming so-called colored regiments, Black soldiers in the army were not treated equally, and sometimes, not even very well. Discovering that Black soldiers were not being fed nutritious meals, forty Black women established the Ladies Committee for the Aid of Sick Soldiers in January 1864, with Williams Garnet named its president. The women took it upon themselves to ensure that Black soldiers got plentiful and nutritious meals. After the war, Williams Garnet continued working to improve the lives of people of color by working with freedmen—newly freed slaves—in the nation's capital city.

Williams Garnet's final home was in Allegheny City, Pennsylvania, located near Pittsburgh. She died there on January 7, 1870. She was fifty-eight years old. Her obituary in the *Christian Recorder* of Nashville, Tennessee, remarked: "Her devotion to the anti-slavery cause, and her sacrifices for the fleeing fugitives, may not be recorded by human pen, but the recording angel has written them."

Her struggle to gain an education in the face of repeated acts of racial hatred and violence no doubt left an indelible mark on Julia Williams Garnet. She remained dedicated throughout her life to advancing the causes of anti-slavery and equality for people of color.

Ona Marie Judge

Choosing Freedom from the Nation's First President

Panel depicting Ona Marie Judge displayed at Independence National Historical Park, Philadelphia. (Courtesy of Eisterhold Associates, Inc. / Exhibited at Independence National Historical Park)

In the spring of 1845, Thomas H. Archibald interviewed an elderly woman living in abject poverty in a small town about five miles inland from the coastal city of Portsmouth, New Hampshire.

The woman, who was likely about seventy years old but estimated by the interviewer to be more than eighty, had lived in New Hampshire as a fugitive slave for nearly fifty years by the time of her conversation with Archibald. As an enslaved person in Virginia, she had dressed in the finest clothes and shoes; her work kept her mostly indoors, performing tasks such as sewing and sorting her mistress's belongings. As a free woman in New Hampshire, she performed backbreaking physical labor as a servant to support herself financially, outlived her husband and all three of her children, and lived in what was described by another interviewer named Benjamin Chase as "a rather obscure place, and in a poor, cold house."

Yet when asked by her interviewers whether she ever wished she had returned to the wealthy Virginia family that legally owned her, she decisively said she preferred freedom in any state to slavery in supposed luxury.

"If asked why she did not remain in her [mistress's] service," Archibald wrote in his article, published in the abolitionist newspaper *The Granite Freeman* of Concord, New Hampshire, on May 22, 1845, "she gives two reasons: first, that she wanted to be *free*; secondly, that she understood that after the decease of her master and mistress, she was to become the property of a granddaughter of theirs, by the name of Custis, and that she was determined never to be *her* slave."

More is now known about this woman named Ona Marie Judge Staines than can be determined about most of those who toiled in obscurity as enslaved people. This is because her legal owners were George and Martha Washington. That she agreed to be interviewed for articles in two abolitionist publications must have been considered quite a coup by the anti-slavery forces of that period.

An article titled "The Remarkable Story of Ona Judge" by Lindsay M. Chervinsky, on the White House Historical Association website, indicates that Judge was born in April 1774 at the Washington country estate of Mount Vernon, outside of Alexandria, Virginia. Her mother was an enslaved housemaid named Betty, and her father a white indentured servant named Andrew Judge. Little is known about her parents' relationship.

Ona Judge was described by the Washingtons as being freckle-faced and having a fairly light complexion. By the time Judge was about ten or twelve years old, Martha Washington was training her as a housemaid and personal assistant. While such a position was likely preferable to working outdoors, planting and harvesting in the hot Virginia sun, the position was still not an easy one for the adolescent Judge. She had to be ready to do whatever her mistress wanted, at any time of day or night. Because she was constantly at Martha Washington's side, both at Mount Vernon and elsewhere, Ona Judge was outfitted in fashionable dresses and shoes.

Ona Judge was among the handful of enslaved people who accompanied the Washingtons when they moved to New York City, when Washington took office as the nation's first president. When the young country's capital was moved to Philadelphia, Judge also accompanied the family there.

In the cities of the North, Judge first encountered sizable populations of free Blacks. The Washingtons also had to come to grips in the North with a growing public attitude against slavery, and a Pennsylvania law that allowed slaves to declare themselves free if they were kept within that state longer than six months. In her book *Never Caught*, Erica Armstrong Dunbar writes about the Washingtons circumventing the law by frequently rotating their slaves' residences back to Mount Vernon.

While a new world opened before Judge in Philadelphia, one impetus for her ultimate decision to flee was the news that Martha Washington intended to bequeath Judge to Washington's granddaughter, Elizabeth Parke Custis, who was said to have a fiery temper.

Judge told interviewer Archibald in 1845, "Whilst they were packing up to go to Virginia, I was packing to go, I didn't know where; for I knew that if I went back to Virginia, I never should get my liberty." Although Judge told her interviewer she was uncertain of the years, it was likely in 1797, as Washington was finishing his second term as president.

In the newspaper articles, Judge said her escape was aided by members of Philadelphia's free Black community. They moved her belongings to the wharves ahead of her arrival, and she then set sail on a ship called the *Nancy*. Once she arrived in Portsmouth, members of the small free Black community there also helped her by housing her and assisting her in gaining employment.

Although Washington's personal viewpoints were turning against slavery as he aged, at the time of his death there were more than 300 enslaved people living and working at Mount Vernon, according to information on the Mount Vernon website. When Washington died in 1799, his will freed the 123 slaves he owned. Another 153 Mount Vernon slaves were owned by the Custis estate, however, and neither George nor Martha had the legal right to free them. Among these so-called "dower slaves" was Ona Marie Judge.

Despite Washington's later decision to free his slaves, at the time Judge fled the Washington household, he and Martha were incredulous she had left. Dunbar, in her book, writes that this attitude was typical of many slaveholders, who viewed themselves as benevolent masters. They simply could not understand the enslaved people's desire for freedom when the planters felt they had treated their enslaved property justly.

As was typical for the time, the Washingtons placed advertisements in the *Philadelphia Gazette* and *Claypoole's American Daily Advertiser*, notifying the public of Judge's escape and offering a reward for her return. Under the headline "Ten Dollars Reward," the ad read, in part, "Absconded from the household of the president of the United States, on Saturday afternoon, Oney Judge, a light Mulatto girl, much freckled, with very black eyes and bushy black hair. . . . As there was no suspicion of her going off, and it happened without the least provocation, it is not easy to conjecture whither she is going—or fully, what her design is."

Judge settled into life in Portsmouth, but just a few months after her arrival, she was recognized on the street by the daughter of Senator John Langdon. Elizabeth Langdon was a friend of one of Martha Washington's granddaughters. When the Washingtons were told of Judge's whereabouts, George Washington wrote for assistance to Secretary of the Treasury Oliver Wolcott Jr., who in turn contacted Joseph Whipple, the customs collector in Portsmouth.

According to an article about Judge on the Boundary Stones web page of WETA, a public radio and television station that serves the Washington, DC, area, Whipple fabricated a story that he was searching for a maid, and Ona Judge replied to the request. During the sham job interview, Whipple tried to convince Judge to return to the Washingtons, and although she initially agreed to do so, she failed to turn up at the wharf to catch the ship that would have returned her to slavery.

Three years later, and after she had married a free Black sailor named John Staines, the Washingtons made another attempt to regain Judge, who was still legally their property. One of Martha's nephews went to Portsmouth to try to convince Judge to return to Virginia with her baby. He also revealed that he would take her by force if necessary.

The Governor John Langdon house in Portsmouth, a site on the Portsmouth Black Heritage Trail. George Washington dined here in 1789, and an enslaved person here is believed to have helped Ona Marie Judge as she sought to remain free. (Courtesy of Cara MacDonald, Cara Mac Media)

Judge was likely aided in avoiding this attempt to return her to slavery by the changing attitudes in New Hampshire. Slavery was disappearing in the Granite State, and by 1805, the small Black population in Portsmouth were all free citizens, according to the Boundary Stones article. In Portsmouth, while Martha's nephew was enjoying the hospitality of the Langdon family—longtime slave owners who had already freed their own slaves—the family, perhaps through a Black servant, sent word for Ona Judge to flee the city and the man who sought to re-enslave her.

She headed inland to the rural community of Greenland, where she would live with the formerly enslaved John Jack and his wife Phillis. She told the interviewer Archibald in 1845 that after George Washington's death in 1799, the Washington family never again tried to force her back into slavery.

Ona Marie Judge Staines's life was far from easy, filled with hard work and emotional heartbreak. When she headed north to freedom in New Hampshire, she knew she would never again see her family members at Mount Vernon. Once in Portsmouth, she lived in poverty, and the jobs she secured demanded difficult physical labor. Her husband was lost at sea in 1803, and her two daughters and son all predeceased her. When she was too old and likely physically broken to work, she and the Jacks' daughters, with whom she lived, received some meager assistance from Rockingham County. She was considered a fugitive until the day she died, in 1848.

Despite all this, she relished her life in New Hampshire as an abolitionist and a Christian. She told her interviewers that her desire for freedom far outweighed any of the hardships she experienced.

Prince Whipple
A Soldier of the Revolution

In 1779, in the midst of the American Revolution, a group of men sent a four-page petition to the New Hampshire Council and House of Representatives. The petition named all the men who signed the document, saying they were "Natives of Africa now forcibly detained in Slavery in said State." It then made a straightforward request: for New Hampshire to abolish slavery within its borders.

The men argued in the petition "that Freedom is an inherent Right of the human Species, not to be surrendered but by Consent for the Sake of social life," and, later in the document, "They, while but Children, and incapable of Self-Defence, whose infancy might have prompted Protection, were seized, imprisoned and transported from their native Country, where (Tho' Ignorance and Inchristianity prevailed), They were born free to a Country, where (Tho' Knowledge, Christianity and Freedom are their Boast), They are compelled, and their unhappy Posterity, to drag on their Lives in miserable Servitude."

The sentiment, if not the words themselves, surely should have been familiar to any supporter of the patriotic cause then playing out in the colonies. The officials who received the petition, however, simply read it and tabled it, taking no action.

Five of the signers were eventually manumitted by their enslavers. The fourteen others died as enslaved men. One of the petitioners who later was freed was Prince Whipple, a man who accompanied his owner William Whipple of Portsmouth, New Hampshire, into service in the American Revolution.

Despite his outward trappings of fashionable clothing, furnished by William Whipple, and the community respect he earned because he could skillfully accomplish any task assigned to him, Prince Whipple was forced to endure a life of indignities and broken promises from the age of ten onward. It was at that age that his father, who was a chief or tribal leader of some note, decided to send his two sons to America to complete their education.

The man who became known as Prince Whipple in New Hampshire was born about 1750 in Ghana, Africa, according to the article "What Freedom Meant to Prince Whipple, the Black Revolutionary Soldier Famous for Rowing Across the Delaware," by historian Timothy Messer-Kruse and published on the Commonplace website that focuses on early American history.

Whipple's father knew another relative who had gone to America, received an education, and returned to Africa, but the arrangement he made for his sons somehow went awry. Cutthroat slave traders sold the boys into slavery, and they ended up as the property of William Whipple, a young New Englander who had participated in the "triangular trade" (a term used to describe the trade routes that connected Europe, the Americas, and Africa during the seventeenth, eighteenth, and nineteenth centuries, predicated on the transatlantic trade of enslaved people).

His years as a mariner earned him enough wealth to leave the sea and settle into a genteel life as a merchant and statesman in Portsmouth, before he was even thirty years old.

As was the custom at the time, enslaved people were given the surnames of their owners, and Prince's first name, not uncommon for an enslaved person, was likely given as a cruel joking reference to his formerly high social status in his native Africa. Prince's brother was given the name Cuffee, another common name for enslaved men.

William Whipple made Prince his so-called manservant, a position that would have required a refined demeanor, and meant that Prince dressed well and attended to the personal needs of his master. This would include preparing William's daily outfits, ensuring his clothes and shoes were brushed and presentable, tending to his horses, and accompanying him on trips.

William Whipple served in the New Hampshire assembly, and Prince accompanied him to Exeter, the colony's capital at the time. Whipple also took Prince with him to Philadelphia, where William Whipple represented New Hampshire in the Continental Congress from 1776 to 1779.

Despite laws that prohibited Blacks from serving in the Continental forces during the Revolution, Prince also joined William in military service, which brought them to battles at Saratoga and in Rhode Island. Some five thousand to eight thousand Black men are believed to have served the Revolutionary cause.

Numerous articles note that William Whipple promised Prince his freedom in return for military service, but reneged on that promise after the war. According to one widely told story, Prince once actually ignored a task William had assigned him, and when William asked Prince about the lapse, Prince said it was because William Whipple was going to fight for freedom, but Prince had no freedom for which to fight.

For many years, Prince Whipple's military service was believed to be immortalized in a famous painting of George Washington crossing the Delaware River on Christmas Day, 1776. In 1851, German American artist Emanuel Leutze painted the work that shows Washington standing near the bow of a small boat being rowed across the river. One of the oarsmen depicted near the bow is Black.

The Black rower in this 1851 oil-on-canvas painting by Emanuel Leutze was long believed to depict Prince Whipple, but more recently it was determined that Whipple could not have been present at the crossing of the Delaware during the American Revolution. (Public Domain / Courtesy of the Metropolitan Museum of Art, New York City)

Historians now say the Black man was not Whipple, as William Whipple was serving in the Continental Congress at the time. Leutze was an abolitionist, and purposefully included a Black soldier in the painting to honor the Revolutionary War service of all Black men, according to information from New York City's Metropolitan Museum of Art, where the painting is now displayed.

In yet another public insult, when printmakers Currier & Ives reproduced the artwork years later during the Jim Crow era, they removed the Black figure from the boat altogether.

While Currier & Ives's action demonstrates that racial prejudice long outlived the formal institution of slavery in the United States, during the Revolutionary War years there were at least some glimmers of changing attitudes.

William Whipple, for example, did make public statements demonstrating his ambivalence about the practice of slavery. At one point while serving in the Continental Congress, William Whipple wrote a letter in response to a proposal to form a regiment of enslaved soldiers from South Carolina: "The last accot's from S. Carolina were favorable. A recommendation is gone thither for raising some regiments of Blacks. This will I suppose lay a foundation for the emancipation of those poor wretches in the Country, & I hope be the means of dispensing the Blessings of freedom to all the Human Race in America." Still, like many other enslavers, intellectual beliefs did not always translate into actual practice, and William Whipple appears to have been reluctant to give his trusted slave freedom.

Back in Portsmouth, Prince Whipple met Dinah Chase, and the couple married on February 22, 1781. The Congregationalist minister who owned her granted her freedom on her wedding day. Prince, however, had to wait three more years before he was finally emancipated by the Whipples.

Dinah and Prince, along with Prince's brother Cuffee, lived in a small house in the rear yard of William Whipple's house. Dinah founded the Ladies Charitable African School and taught Black children out of their home. The couple also had seven of their own children.

Both Prince and his brother Cuffee were valuable members of the Portsmouth community. Cuffee was a talented musician, and Prince was a regular at most society events in Portsmouth. "He was the Caleb Quotem of the old-fashioned semi-monthly assemblies, and at all large weddings and dinners, balls and evening parties, nothing could go on right without Prince," according to an account quoted in an article titled "Prince Whipple, Soldier of the American Revolution" by Bill Belton, published in JSTOR, an online library of scholarly works. (Caleb Quotem, a character in a nineteenth-century play called *The Review*, was a master of numerous professions.)

When William Whipple died in 1785, Prince Whipple's family continued to live in the small house behind the mansion, now known as the Moffatt-Ladd House in Portsmouth. Prince Whipple remained in the house until he died at age forty-six, in 1796. Dinah remained there until William Whipple's widow died, and the house was inherited by the Whipple children. That generation decided to relocate Dinah to a house located in a neighborhood occupied by more Black residents.

Although William Whipple, along with Prince and Dinah Whipple, are all buried in Portsmouth's North Cemetery, even in death the Black couple was treated quite differently than their white contemporaries. William Whipple has a large monument marking his grave, while those of Prince and Dinah were unmarked. Years after his death, local veterans paid for a small white monument to mark Prince's grave. Dinah's remains unmarked.

One final irony is the fact that William Whipple's cemetery monument notes his "universal benevolence." Clearly, the story of his relationship with Prince Whipple demonstrates that when it came to enslaving other humans, William Whipple's benevolence had some decided limitations.

Prince Whipple and his brother Cuffee were granted lifelong use of this plot of land on High Street in Portsmouth after they were emancipated in the 1780s. Known as the Black Whipple House, it is now a site on the Portsmouth Black Heritage Trail. (Photo by Cara MacDonald, Cara Mac Media)

Harriet Wilson
An Author Who Struggled to Survive

In an early chapter of the book *Our Nig*, members of the Bellmont family debate the fate of a young child who was abandoned at their house. While the husband, described in the book as "a kind, humane man, who would not grudge hospitality to the poorest wanderer, nor fail to sympathize with any sufferer," was inclined to keep and care for the child, his wife was a harsh, cruel woman, and he was reluctant to go against her wishes.

The mother and her children have this conversation:

> *"Send her to the county house," said Mary, in reply to the query what should be done with her, in a tone which indicated self-importance in the speaker. She was indeed the idol of her mother, and more nearly resembled her in disposition and manners than the others.*
>
> *Jane, an invalid daughter, the eldest of those at home, was reclining on a sofa, apparently uninterested.*
>
> *"Keep her," said Jack. "She's real handsome and bright, and not very black either."*
>
> *"Yes," rejoined Mary; "that's just like you, Jack. She'll be of no use at all these three years, right under foot all the time."*
>
> *"Poh, Miss Mary; if she should stay, it wouldn't be two days before you would be telling the girls about our nig, our nig!" retorted Jack.*
>
> *"I don't want a nigger 'round me, do you, mother?" asked Mary.*
>
> *"I don't mind the nigger in the child. I should like a dozen better than one," replied her mother. "If I could make her do my work in a few years, I would keep her. I have so much trouble with girls I hire, I am almost persuaded if I have one to train up in my way from a*

child, I shall be able to keep them awhile. I am tired of changing every few months."

"Where could she sleep?" asked Mary. "I don't want her near me."

"In the L chamber," answered the mother.

"How'll she get there?" asked Jack. "She'll be afraid to go through that dark passage, and she can't climb the ladder safely."

"She'll have to go there; it's good enough for a nigger," was the reply.

The book *Our Nig*, published in 1859 with its brazen racist term right in the title, was written by Harriet E. Wilson. Widely believed to be autobiographical, the conversation with its degrading references to a young, Black child, is apparently typical of ones Wilson herself heard. The novel's main character is Frado, a mixed-race girl abandoned by her mother and forced into indentured servitude with the Bellmonts, to be severely abused by Mrs. Bellmont.

The novel clearly follows the trajectory of Wilson's own life, and pointedly calls out the contradictions of an abolitionist movement laser-focused on ending Southern slavery, but often blind to the abuses lodged against free Blacks living in Northern states, and unsympathetic to those who fought for equal rights among the races.

Wilson is now credited with writing one of the earliest books by an African American, but her work was all but forgotten for many decades. It was rediscovered in the early 1980s by Henry Louis Gates Jr., the host of the popular PBS television series *Finding Your Roots*, and the director of the Hutchins Center for African and African American Research at Harvard University. Gates came across a copy of the novel while browsing in a rare book store in New York City. Gates and others delved into researching the book, identifying Wilson as its author, then researching her life. Much like the story of her character Frado, they discovered a rather tragic tale.

Wilson was born in 1825 as Harriet E. Adams, often called Hattie, in Milford, New Hampshire. Milford is on the Souhegan River in southern New Hampshire, and was the home of granite quarries and textile mills. In the nineteenth century, it also became a locus of abolitionist sentiment. In January 1843, an anti-slavery convention was held there that was attended by many of the most notable abolitionists of the day. The First Congregational Church in Milford supported the anti-slavery cause, and in 1844 invited representatives of all churches in the county to meet to discuss what action could be taken against the institution of slavery. The town also was home to an abolitionist singing troupe known as the Hutchinson Family Singers.

Amid all the abolitionist sentiment, Harriet Adams lived in poverty, almost anonymously as one of just a handful of Black residents in town. Her mother was a white washerwoman who abandoned her when she was only about five or six years old. Her father, who was Black, died when she was about three. Harriet worked as an indentured servant until sometime between 1843 and 1846, according to information from The Harriet Wilson Project, an organization that seeks to educate the public about Wilson, promoting reading and discussions about her book.

Between 1847 and 1850, Harriet Adams is listed as a pauper by the town. She boarded with other residents and worked for them as a servant. Toward the end of 1850, she moved to Massachusetts, and the following year married a man named Thomas Wilson back in Milford, New Hampshire. But by 1852, she was living at the Hillsborough County Poor Farm in Goffstown, New Hampshire. Her only child, a son named George, was born there.

Although her husband returned to reclaim his family, the reunion was short-lived. He died aboard a sloop in Cuba in 1853, and Wilson was forced to place her child in foster care while she traveled to a variety of locations in Massachusetts and New Hampshire, searching for a way to make a living to support herself and George. She battled ill-health as she struggled to work as a servant, a seamstress, and selling hair products.

She wrote *Our Nig* in an effort to survive. It was published in Boston by the firm of George C. Rand and Avery. Rand was himself an abolitionist. While the author was anonymous when the book was first published, Wilson did write in the preface about her desire to retrieve her son: "Deserted by kindred, disabled by failing health, I am forced to some experiment which shall aid me in maintaining myself and [my] child without extinguishing this feeble life." Unfortunately, her efforts did not help her son. He died of a fever in the poorhouse just six months after the book was published.

While her book certainly was critical of Northern white society, including abolitionists who did little to improve the lives of their struggling Black neighbors, Wilson was not an overt activist or anti-slavery speaker. Instead, she became involved with spiritualism, a popular movement in the mid-nineteenth century. Spiritualists believed, among other things, that communication with the spirits of dead people was possible.

In 1867, according to information from The Harriet Wilson Project, Wilson was described as "the eloquent and earnest colored trance medium" in *The Banner of Light*, a Boston spiritualist newspaper. In the years just following the Civil War, she attended and spoke at spiritualist gatherings and lectured—sometimes, when said to be in a trance—in Massachusetts, Maine, New Hampshire, and Connecticut.

By 1870, Wilson was living in Boston. She got married again to a man named John Robinson, who was an apothecary. The 1870 federal census lists both she and her husband as physicians, according to information from The Harriet Wilson Project.

While she spent her later years most active as a spiritualist and is not known to have ever had any more written work published, her legacy in spreading the story of the struggles of free Blacks in the North has now been hailed and preserved. In the fall of 2006, the Harriet E. Wilson Memorial was installed in Bicentennial Park in Milford, New Hampshire. A sculpture depicting Wilson has her carrying her book in an outstretched hand while she seeks to shield the figure of a young boy at her left side.

JerriAnne Boggis, founder and director of The Harriet Wilson Project, told NPR in an article published in 2020: "Some of the things she wrote in her book were shocking. But it's not any more shocking than anything that you didn't know about slavery. It was shocking that it happened in the North, because that's not our story. Our story is the abolitionist movement."

Harriet Wilson died on June 28, 1900, in Quincy, Massachusetts. Her cause of death was listed as inanition, defined as "exhaustion from lack of nourishment."

This sculpture honoring Harriet E. Wilson was installed in 2006 in Bicentennial Park in Milford, New Hampshire, the town in which she lived. (Photo by Cara MacDonald, Cara Mac Media)

New York
Site of Bloody, Racially Motivated Riots and a Community of Black Intellectuals

More than sixty years before revolutionary fervor overtook the American colonies and led to their independence, a group of enslaved people living in New York City rose up to fight for their own independence. The New York City slave revolt of 1712—one of the earliest slave uprisings in America—occurred at a time when about one thousand of the six thousand to eight thousand people then living in the city were enslaved.

The event unfolded in this manner. A group of African-born enslaved residents encouraged their compatriots to revolt against their owners, setting fire to an outhouse to signal others to join their effort. The revolt was relatively short-lived, however, and ended badly for the enslaved. The militia, joined by armed white residents, brutally put down the uprising. While nine whites were killed and six of the enslaved committed suicide rather than face certain torture, some forty slaves were brought to trial.

Some were acquitted, but more were executed, and some in particularly brutal manners. According to Britannica, four were burned alive; one was crushed by a wheel; one was starved to death while kept in chains; and a pregnant woman was kept alive until her baby was born and then she was executed. Most were hanged. The revolt also resulted in much stricter rules governing the enslaved, including allowing slaveholders to mete out very harsh punishments.

This early revolt in a Northern colony is one event in the long and complex story of slavery and abolition in New York. Although later generations would believe slavery hardly existed in this place, the institution has deep roots in New York.

Slaves were first brought to New Amsterdam—what would become New York City—by the Dutch West Indies Company in 1626. The first slave auction was held in New Amsterdam in 1655. By 1703, the city had the second-highest proportion of enslaved humans in the colonies. It was second only to Charleston, South Carolina, and some 42 percent of the population were slaveholders.

Enslaved Africans worked as domestic servants, farmers, and laborers. They built roads, forts, walls, docks, churches, taverns, and the first city hall, according to information from the New York Historical (Society). The city's Common Council in the colonial period also passed numerous regulations governing the lives of Blacks, including prohibiting them from owning property, forbidding them from venturing out at night or past certain geographic limitations, and making it illegal for more than three Blacks to congregate for social or other gatherings.

During the Revolution, New York City was occupied by the British, and they offered Blacks their freedom in return for fighting for the British cause. After the war, the British evacuated some three thousand enslaved individuals, resettling many of them as freedmen in Nova Scotia.

As soon as the Revolution gave way to the establishment of a new nation, organizations advocating for abolition were established. The New York Manumission Society was formed in 1785 and included such influential members as Alexander Hamilton and John Jay. A gradual manumission law was passed in 1799, but slavery would not be abolished in New York until 1827.

At the time calls for abolition were increasing in the early nineteenth century, the landscape for Black New Yorkers was varied. In 1821, the New York legislature decided that Black male New Yorkers could vote, but only if they had at least $250 in property. No such property stipulation was imposed on white male voters.

New York's economy was inextricably intertwined with the institution of slavery in businesses such as banking, insurance, the law, and maritime industries. New York City mariners continued to participate in the slave trade even after that action was outlawed. While there was a large free Black community in the city, it remained a dangerous place for the many residents of color, as racially motivated violence frequently flared and slave hunters roamed the streets.

People such as the fearless David Ruggles, a founder in 1835 of the New York Committee of Vigilance, prowled the docks on the lookout for the enslaved who were seeking freedom in the North, as well as slaves who were being brought to the city illegally. Frederick Douglass, who escaped slavery in Maryland and made his way to New York City, was first assisted by Ruggles. In 1848, Douglass made his way to Rochester, where he would publish his abolitionist newspaper, *The North Star*.

The growing abolition movement took root throughout Upstate New York, and the area became one of the prime centers for abolitionist thought and sentiment in the country. The New York Anti-Slavery Society was established in 1835 in Peterboro. Educational institutions such as the integrated Oneida Institute in Whitestown educated many top Black intellectuals, including Henry Highland Garnet.

Even in the parts of the state where abolitionist sentiment was the strongest, however, Blacks were not safe from capture by slave hunters. Solomon Northup, a free man who lived in Saratoga Springs, was lured away by dishonest men who promised him lucrative employment. Northup was drugged and sold into slavery in Louisiana, where he would spend twelve brutal years. He regained his freedom only after successfully sending word of his capture to a white friend in New York.

In New York City in the years just prior to the Civil War, Blacks continued to face violent incidents, harassment, and segregation even as institutions such as Horace Greeley's abolitionist and progressive newspaper, the *New-York Tribune*, was gaining in influence. With a large influx of European immigrants into the city, however, tensions grew between these new residents trying to establish themselves and their Black neighbors, who often were vying for the same jobs.

The passage of an 1863 federal law that instituted a draft for the Union military touched off some of the worst racial violence in New York City history. Poor white residents, many of whom were Irish immigrants, were outraged by the military conscription that also allowed wealthier residents to hire a substitute to complete their military service for them, or pay $300 to allow them to opt out of service. The law touched off what would come to be known as the New York City Draft Riots in July 1863, five days of horrendous violence that left more than one hundred Black men dead, although unofficial counts indicate the riots may have claimed the lives of more than a thousand.

The rioting mob lynched Blacks, set fire to houses and businesses, destroyed an orphanage housing Black children, and attacked Greeley's newspaper office. Many Black residents fled Manhattan, never to return. Following the Civil War, according to information from the Museum of the City of New York, the city remained a segregated place for many decades.

Still, collective memory seems incredibly short. By 1991, when a construction project in Lower Manhattan unearthed an African burial ground dating to the mid-1630s, many contemporary residents were shocked to learn of their city's ties to slavery, racial oppression, and segregation. The African Burial Ground National Monument established at that sacred site now attracts some fifty thousand visitors annually.

Henry Highland Garnet
Called for the Enslaved to Throw Off Oppressors

Henry Highland Garnet. Creative Commons. (Public Domain / Courtesy of National Portrait Gallery, Smithsonian Institution)

In August 1843, Henry Highland Garnet stood before the National Negro Convention in Buffalo, New York, and delivered a speech that shocked the delegates there. Only a year earlier, Garnet had said he believed that white Americans held the primary responsibility for abolishing slavery. Now, however, his words showed he had had a dramatic change of heart on the subject.

In the speech, Garnet first criticized Northern abolitionists for being long on talk and short on action. Their efforts, after all, had done little to end the practice of slavery. As he spoke on that August day, he pointed out some of the evils of slavery: "Two hundred and twenty-seven years ago, the first of our injured race were brought to the shores of America. They came not with glad spirits to select their homes in the New World. They came not with their own consent, to find an unmolested enjoyment of the blessings of this fruitful soil. The first dealings they had with men calling themselves Christians, exhibited to them the worst features of corrupt and sordid hearts; and convinced them that no cruelty is too great, no villainy and no robbery too abhorrent for even enlightened men to perform, when influenced by avarice and lust."

Later in the speech, he turned his attention to the enslaved, saying,

NEITHER GOD, NOR ANGELS, OR JUST MEN, COMMAND YOU TO SUFFER FOR A SINGLE MOMENT. THEREFORE, IT IS YOUR SOLEMN AND IMPERATIVE DUTY TO USE EVERY MEANS, BOTH MORAL, INTELLECTUAL, AND PHYSICAL, THAT PROMISES SUCCESS.

Garnet used examples of other slave uprisings, both successful and unsuccessful, to make his point. He invoked the names of Joseph Cinque, who led a successful uprising aboard the ship *Amistad*; Toussaint L'Ouverture, one of the leaders of Haiti's revolutionary slave uprising; and Nat Turner, who led an 1831 slave revolt in Virginia that left 55 whites and some 120 Blacks dead.

Garnet's message was clear: Without resistance from the enslaved themselves, white enslavers would be unlikely to ever end the institution upon which so much of the American economy relied. He said, "Brethren, arise, arise! Strike for your lives and liberties. Now is the day and the hour. Let every slave throughout the land do this and the days of slavery are numbered. You cannot be more oppressed than you have been—you cannot suffer greater cruelties than you have already. *Rather die freemen than live to be slaves.* Remember that you are FOUR MILLIONS!"

Besides setting the delegates' heads spinning and their tongues wagging, Garnet's speech and stance were debated at length by the convention. Delegates ultimately refused to endorse the action Garnet urged. It was too radical, they said. The vote to reject, however, was made by the narrowest of margins—a single vote.

Within about a decade, more abolitionists would come to believe Garnet's call for slave resistance was a sound strategy. His words also were said to inspire John Brown's 1859 raid on the federal arsenal at Harpers Ferry, Virginia, an action that failed in its pursuit to spur a mass slave uprising.

Henry Highland Garnet knew something about the dehumanizing institution of slavery firsthand. He was born into slavery in 1815 in New Market, Maryland, located about forty miles northwest of Washington, DC. When Garnet was about nine years old, his parents were granted permission by their enslaver's family to attend a funeral. This occurred shortly after their enslaver's death. The family used that opportunity to escape to the North via the Underground Railroad, according to information from the New York Historical (Society).

The family settled in New York City, where Garnet attended the African Free School. It was a school where Black boys had a tremendous amount of educational success. Many Black activists and intellectuals graduated from the institution, including James McCune Smith, who would become a lifelong friend of Garnet's. While he was a student at the African Free School, Garnet and some of his friends in 1834 formed the Garrison Literary and Benevolent Association, named for the famous abolitionist William Lloyd Garrison. Some 150 Black youth attended the group's first meeting.

Garnet, as did many young Black men in the time period, worked as a mariner as a young teenager. After one trip at sea, he returned to New York to discover that slave hunters had sought to ensnare his family.

While his parents escaped, some sources indicate Garnet's sister was captured. Whether or not she was, what is certain is that Garnet armed himself with a knife and prowled the streets of Manhattan, seeking revenge against the slave catchers, until friends convinced him to leave the city and go into temporary hiding on Long Island.

In 1835, seeking to complete his education, Garnet went to New Hampshire to attend Noyes Academy in Canaan. There, he met his future wife, Julia Ward Williams, who also was a student there. Their education was cut short, however, when the school was literally destroyed by an anti-abolitionist mob that dragged the building off its foundation and down the road. Before that final destructive act, Garnet is said to have heroically defended the school and its students by firing at the white attackers and allowing the students time to escape the violence.

Garnet and the other Noyes Academy students were then left to search for an alternative place to complete their educations. Garnet headed to Oneida Institute in New York, as did Julia Ward Williams. Garnet graduated from Oneida in 1839, and he and Williams married in 1841. The couple would have three children, but only one survived to adulthood.

After completing school, Garnet became a minister. He also taught Black children at a school in Troy, New York. In 1842, he was ordained in Troy and became the first pastor of the Liberty Street Presbyterian Church. He also became more active in fighting against slavery during this time period.

Garnet continued to espouse more radical views following the Buffalo convention. He came to support the colonization movement that would relocate Black Americans to Liberia. In 1859, he founded the African Civilization Society.

Garnet only narrowly escaped death during the 1863 New York City Draft Riots, in which rampaging white residents, many of them Irish immigrants, targeted Blacks with violence. The root cause was the contemporary practice allowing wealthy men to pay to avoid military service for the Union during the Civil War, but racial hatred was also fanned by the belief that freed slaves would flood Northern cities and compete with poor whites for jobs. Garnet's views were well-known, and he was targeted by the marauding mob.

In 1864, Garnet moved to Washington, DC, where he became pastor of the Fifteenth Street Presbyterian Church. The next year, President Lincoln invited him to address the House of Representatives, where he spoke in favor of the Thirteenth Amendment to abolish slavery—the first Black American to address Congress. Garnet titled his sermon "Let the Monster Perish." In it, he recalled some of his firsthand experiences as an enslaved child: "The first sight that met my eyes was a Christian mother enslaved by professed Christians, but thank God, now a saint in heaven. The first sounds that startled my ear and sent a shudder through my soul were the cracking of the whip and the clanking of chains."

In 1881, Garnet was appointed to a position that was the equivalent of ambassador to Liberia by President James Garfield. Although Garnet had always dreamed of traveling to Africa, his time there proved very short. After just two months in the country, Garnet died of malaria there. He was given a state funeral by the Liberian government and was buried in the capital city of Monrovia.

Elizabeth Jennings Graham
Led Fight to Desegregate Public Transportation

Elizabeth Jennings Graham from July 1895 edition of *The American Women's Journal*. (Kansas Historical Society)

Elizabeth Jennings was simply trying to get to church on a hot July day. For a Black woman in 1850s New York City, however, using public transportation was not so simple. What was supposed to be a short trip to the First Colored American Congregational Church instead turned into a prolonged struggle that resulted in her making history.

Horse-drawn streetcars were all privately owned in New York City in the mid-nineteenth century. As such, the decision of whether or not to allow passengers of color to ride was often up to the whims of the lines' owners. Some cars displayed signs indicating that passengers of color were allowed to board. Even so, most Black residents of the city at that time usually chose to walk to their destinations rather than risk being subjected to drivers' racist insults.

On this particular steamy day, however, Jennings was determined to use the Third Avenue streetcar because she was running late. So, the young teacher and church organist boarded the segregated streetcar at the corner of Pearl and Chatham streets in Lower Manhattan, not far from the piers along the East River. The conductor, however, ordered her off the vehicle.

She refused.

Three days later, under a headline reading "Outrage Upon Colored Citizens," Horace Greeley's progressive and abolitionist newspaper, the *New York Daily Tribune*, reported about the incident. Jennings provided the information that was included in the article, saying the conductor of the streetcar she boarded told her to disembark and wait for the next car, because it had "her people" on it. She said she didn't have any people and simply wanted to get to church.

When the next car pulled up, one that did allow people of color to ride, it was too full to board, so Jennings stood her ground with the original conductor. He then indicated she might ride only if no other white passenger objected. She said, "I told him I was a respectable person, born and raised in New York . . . and that he was a good-for-nothing, impudent fellow for insulting decent persons on their way to church."

The war of words then turned physical. The conductor and driver grabbed Jennings and struggled to literally throw her off the vehicle. She screamed and protested, but the two men succeeded, and Jennings ended up bruised, battered, and in the street. Although she didn't know it then, she would ultimately prevail in her quest for the right to ride public transportation without fear of being physically extricated.

At the time of the incident, which occurred when Elizabeth Jennings was about twenty-four years old, she was already well acquainted with activism. She was both wealthy and educated, and came from a family dedicated to advocating for abolition and Black civil rights. Her father was Thomas L. Jennings, a tailor who was the earliest known Black American to hold a patent (for a dry-cleaning process), according to information from the Museum of the City of New York. Thomas Jennings's success as a tailor earned him financial stability and the ability to support abolitionist causes. He also was a leader in the National Colored Convention movement and one of the founders of New York's Abyssinian Baptist Church.

Elizabeth Jennings's mother was a woman named Elizabeth Cartwright. She was a writer and founding member of the Ladies Literary Society of New York. Among that group's causes was helping those who escaped slavery.

After the July 16, 1854, streetcar incident and the resulting protests by the Black community, Elizabeth Jennings decided to sue the Third Avenue Railway Company, along with the specific conductor and driver involved in throwing her into the street. Her lawyer was a twenty-four-year-old man named Chester A. Arthur. A Vermont native, Arthur was a member of the New York law firm of Erastus D. Culver, and an abolitionist. The firm had successfully argued in the *Lemmon v. New York* case that slaves brought to New York by their owners were automatically freed because the state prohibited slavery.

Arthur was given much credit for the success of the *Lemmon* case, and he also was successful in arguing on behalf of Elizabeth Jennings. The judge ruled that "colored persons, if sober, well-behaved, and free from disease" had all the same rights to ride public transportation as any other person. She was awarded $250 in damages, and the railroad company was ordered to desegregate, marking the first case in American history of court-ordered desegregation on public transportation. Her case also paved the way for the establishment of the Legal Rights Association, a group that fought against segregation in public transportation.

Arthur would go on to become much better known as the twenty-first president of the United States, ascending from the position of vice president in 1881, upon the assassination of James Garfield.

Unfortunately, Jennings's victory in the case did not desegregate all New York City public transportation. The case applied only to the Third Avenue Railroad Company. By 1860, however, all of the city's streetcars and railcars were desegregated.

Despite this victory, Jennings's life would be marked by some personal setbacks and racial prejudice. She married Charles Graham in the late 1850s, but the couple's only child, a son, died when he was just a year old, during the height of the violence against Blacks that occurred in the 1863 New York City Draft Riots. More than one hundred Black residents were killed in the riots, with thousands left homeless.

Elizabeth and Charles Graham moved to New Jersey in an effort to escape the racist-fueled rampages. Jennings Graham eventually moved back to Manhattan in the late 1860s, after her husband died.

Jennings Graham's determination to help people of color in New York City continued to be a force in her life. She had been a teacher since at least 1849, and, much later, helped to found the first kindergarten in the city for Black children, operating it out of her home on West 41st Street. The school operated from 1895 until Jennings Graham's death in 1901. An article in *American Woman's Journal* described the school this way: "The children are developing sense-knowledge, and learning to exercise that self-activity which lies at the root of this admirable system. . . . A yard connected with the house in which the school is situated has been carefully prepared, where the little ones have planted seeds and roots, and where they have an opportunity to exercise and play." The kindergarten was a fitting culmination for Jennings Graham's long and notable career as an educator and reformer as she continued to help imbue self-respect and a love of learning in her students.

In 1859, not long after the streetcar incident, Frederick Douglass said of Elizabeth Jennings Graham that she was "the most learned of our female teachers in the city of New York, having obtained mainly through her own labor, the honor of a diploma from the Board of Education of said city."

Elizabeth Jennings Graham died on June 5, 1901, at her home of complications from Bright's disease, at around seventy-five years of age. She was buried in Cypress Hills Cemetery in Brooklyn, the same cemetery where her son was laid to rest.

Solomon Northup
Born Free, Kidnapped into Slavery

Solomon Northup's life story is evidence of the precarious existence of all Black Americans in the nineteenth century. Although he grew into adulthood as a free man, that fact did not prevent him from being kidnapped and sold into slavery. Despite working hard throughout his adult life, societal restrictions preventing Blacks from entering most professions meant he often struggled financially. While he carried legal documentation showing that he was free, when his papers were stolen from him, no one would take the word of a Black man to investigate his legal status. Even though his father was emancipated from the white family whose last name the families shared, Solomon Northup ultimately required the assistance of a white Northup to regain his freedom. And although Northup sought justice after his twelve-year ordeal as a slave, the men who kidnapped him were never punished for their crimes, in part because of the legal limbo Black Americans found themselves entangled in following the 1857 US Supreme Court decision in *Dred Scott v. Sandford*, in which the court ruled that Black men, free or enslaved, were not American citizens.

Northup and the horrors of his life story became well-known to Americans through his 1853 book *Twelve Years a Slave*, written with the help of a ghostwriter shortly after he was freed from the Louisiana plantation to which he had been sold. Some thirty thousand copies of the book sold after it was published, and it is credited with helping fan the flames of the abolition movement that was at that point moving the country toward civil war.

The lead-in page to Solomon Northup's book, *Twelve Years a Slave*. (The Historic New Orleans Collection / Williams Research Center)

It wasn't long, however, before Northup and his terrible tale were forgotten by the public. It remained that way until the rediscovery of his story in 1999, when a Saratoga Springs educator named Renee Moore and the city of Saratoga Springs erected a historic marker in his honor. The city also began celebrating Solomon Northup Day each July. A short time later, his story became much more widely known when the award-winning film *12 Years a Slave* was released in 2013.

Northup's life began quietly enough, and remained that way until he reached adulthood. He was born in the tiny Adirondacks town of Minerva, New York, in 1807 or 1808. At the time of his birth, the town was called Schroon. Mintus Northup, Solomon's father, was born into slavery, but was granted his freedom upon the death of his enslaver,

Captain Henry Northup. Mintus Northup was able to buy his own farm, and the Black Northups maintained an amicable relationship with the white Northups, a relationship that later would prove fortuitous for Solomon.

Solomon wrote this about his father in his book:

Though born a slave, and laboring under the disadvantages to which my unfortunate race is subjected, my father was a man respected for his industry and integrity, as many now living, who well remember him, are ready to testify. His whole life was passed in the peaceful pursuits of agriculture, never seeking employment in those more menial positions, which seem to be especially allotted to the children of Africa. Besides giving us an education surpassing that ordinarily bestowed upon children in our condition, he acquired, by his diligence and economy, a sufficient property qualification to entitle him to the right of suffrage.

Northup grew up working on his family's farm. He married Anne Hampton in 1829, and in 1834, the couple moved to the growing resort town of Saratoga Springs. While Black men such as Northup would find it relatively easy to find employment there in the service industry during the busy summer season, the slower winter months left them scrambling to make a living. Northup performed a variety of odd jobs, and likely found it difficult to support his family financially in the lean months.

Northup did develop a reputation as a talented fiddler, however, and it was this skill that brought him to the attention of two congenial, but dishonest, men in March 1841. With compliments and the promise of a lucrative payout for playing in their so-called circus, Northup agreed to travel with the men. The trio went first to New York City, and then traveled on to Washington, DC, where slavery was still legal. There Northup was drugged by his traveling companions, and the documents attesting to his status as a free man were stolen. He woke up shackled and alone in a dark cell inside the Williams Slave Pen, located near what is now Seventh Street and Independence Avenue, not far from L'Enfant Plaza.

When a man entered the cell and told Northup he would be sold at a slave market in New Orleans, Northup protested, saying he was a free man from New York. For his honesty, he was savagely beaten. Northup later recalled in his book: "I prayed for mercy, but my prayer was only answered with imprecations and with stripes. I thought I must die beneath the lashes of the accursed brute. Even now the flesh crawls upon my bones, as I recall the scene. I was all on fire. My sufferings I can compare to nothing else than the burning agonies of hell!"

He was later shipped to New Orleans, given a new name, and for the next twelve years was forced to work on cotton and sugar plantations in central Louisiana. His wife and family in New York had no idea where he was or what had happened to him. His ordeal was not unique in antebellum America. Many instances of illegal seizures of free Blacks being sold into slavery are documented, and it's presumed by historians that thousands likely occurred.

In Louisiana, Northup tried various times to reclaim his freedom and return to the North. He sent one letter north shortly after he arrived in the state, but because he couldn't identify where he was, no one was able to come to his rescue. He also sought ways to escape, but never succeeded.

In *Twelve Years a Slave*, Northup describes in horrifying detail the barbarity of a Louisiana slave market:

> Next day many customers called to examine Freeman's "new lot." The latter gentleman was very loquacious, dwelling at much length upon our several good points and qualities. He would make us hold up our heads, walk briskly back and forth, while customers would feel of our hands and arms and bodies, turn us about, ask us what we could do, make us open our mouths and show our teeth, precisely as a jockey examines a horse which he is about to barter for or purchase. Sometimes a man or woman was taken back to the small house in the yard, stripped, and inspected more minutely. Scars upon a slave's back were considered evidence of a rebellious or unruly spirit, and hurt his sale.

Solomon Northup helped build this house for Edwin Epps while wrongly enslaved in Louisiana. Originally built on Bayou Boeuf, it was later moved to Bunkie, Louisiana, and again, to Alexandria, Louisiana. (Photo by John H. Lawrence, The Historic New Orleans Collection / Williams Research Center)

Northup also resisted his enslavers, fighting back when they sought to whip him and narrowly escaping lynching for these actions. He was rescued by an overseer of William Prince Ford, Northup's original Louisiana enslaver, a man Northup described as kind and fair despite being a slave owner.

Northup vividly describes the terrible abuses of slavery in his book, one passage illustrating the special torment endured by some female slaves. Northup writes about Patsey, an enslaved woman who was especially strong and an able field hand:

Yet Patsey wept oftener, and suffered more, than any of her companions. She had been literally excoriated. Her back bore the scars of a thousand stripes; not because she was backward in her work, nor because she was of an unmindful and rebellious spirit, but because it had fallen to her lot to be the slave of a licentious master and a jealous mistress. She shrank before the lustful eye of the one, and was in danger even of her life at the hands of the other, and between the two, she was indeed accursed. In the great house, for days together, there were high and angry words, poutings and estrangement, whereof she was the innocent cause. Nothing delighted the mistress so much as to see her suffer, and more than once, when Epps had refused to sell her, has she tempted me with bribes to put her secretly to death, and bury her body in some lonely place in the margin of the swamp.

After nearly twelve years in slavery, Northup met a Canadian carpenter named Samuel Bass, hired by Northup's enslaver Edwin Epps to build a new house. When Northup learned Bass had anti-slavery sympathies, Northup convinced Bass to mail a letter on his behalf to Henry B. Northup, the nephew of the white man who had enslaved Northup's father. Henry Northup came to Louisiana to search for Solomon Northup—a difficult task, because Solomon's name had been changed. Henry Northup finally succeeded in locating Solomon Northup and helped him reclaim his freedom and return to New York.

Solomon Northup returned to New York in 1853, at the age of forty-four. With the assistance of a white lawyer and writer named David Wilson, Northup released the memoir of his time in captivity that same year. Northup became a sought-after speaker at abolitionist meetings and events following the book's release.

He was not as successful in bringing his kidnappers to justice. In Washington, DC, he brought charges against the man who had imprisoned him and sold him in the South, but the case was dismissed in part because Northup was barred from testifying—because he was Black. In 1854, the men he'd met in Saratoga Springs—who tricked him into joining them to play his fiddle—were identified and indicted. After years of legal finagling, including arguments over jurisdiction and uncertainty caused by the *Dred Scott* decision, the case against the men was dismissed in 1857.

Although his book and his speeches made him a national celebrity of sorts, Northup's fame was relatively short-lived. He is believed to have worked for a time on the Underground Railroad, but what became of him in his final years is a mystery. One of the final news accounts about Northup was published in 1857, when he was prevented by an anti-abolitionist crowd from telling his story in a public speech in Canada. By about 1863, Northup had all but disappeared from public view, and researchers seeking some sort of paper trail from his later years have come up empty. No death or burial records have been located.

Some descendants and friends of Northup's believed he was kidnapped a second time, but most scholars think he simply died at a fairly young age. If he died around 1863, he would have been about fifty-five years old.

James McCune Smith
Abolitionist, Physician, and Pharmacist

Portrait of James McCune Smith, created by artist Melissa Moshetti for his induction into the National Abolition Hall of Fame and Museum. (Courtesy of National Abolition Hall of Fame and Museum)

While in New York City during his thirteen-month Farewell to America tour in 1824–1825, the Marquis de Lafayette asked to visit the African Free School No. 2, located on Mulberry Street in Lower

Manhattan. An abolitionist himself, the Revolutionary War hero was interested in the exceptional education the school provided to boys of color, and is said to have regretted helping establish a country where slavery was legal.

During the visit, one boy in the outstanding group of scholars at the school was chosen to address Lafayette. That boy was eleven-year-old James McCune Smith. His exceptional intellectual abilities would continue to set him apart throughout his lifetime. He was the first Black American to earn a medical degree, the first to run a pharmacy, and always among the top Black intellectuals in the country. He also was an activist who used his education to refute popular beliefs among antebellum Americans that Blacks did not have the same intellectual capacity as did whites.

Smith was a member of the American Anti-Slavery Society, worked with Frederick Douglass to start the National Council of Colored People in 1853, and was active in the Committee of Thirteen that formed to fight against the Fugitive Slave Act of 1850. Smith also was a member of a radical abolitionist group advocating an immediate end to slavery, through the use of violence if necessary. That group included Douglass and John Brown, who is best known for his ill-fated 1859 attack on the federal arsenal at Harpers Ferry, Virginia (now West Virginia), which Brown hoped would trigger a slave rebellion.

Douglass, one of the country's top abolitionist orators, called Smith "the single most important influence" on his life. Indeed, Smith's accomplishments should have been seen as clear-cut evidence of the amazing potential of all Black Americans, given that he was born enslaved in 1813 and overcame numerous racist challenges in his life to achieve great success.

Not many details of Smith's earliest childhood and family background are known. His mother was enslaved in Charleston, South Carolina, and moved north to New York City at some point. His father was a white man, but Smith may not have known who that man was. In one of Smith's articles, he indicated he had family members in the South, and among them were both slaves and slaveholders.

Smith was still enslaved when he became a pupil at the African Free School. He was emancipated in 1827, when New York formally freed any remaining enslaved people living in the state. Smith recalled the celebrations in the Black community on July 5, one day after the official emancipation date, to differentiate it from the July 4 holiday.

The African Free School employed an unusual teaching methodology under which the boys seemed to blossom. The white headmaster of the school essentially made all the students teaching assistants; learning from each other, they spurred on and encouraged great successes among their peers. The school helped to produce a large number of the top Black intellectuals and reformers of the time period.

After graduating at age fifteen, Smith set his sights on higher education—specifically, medical school. Because of the pervasive racism in the country, however, he was refused admission to the two New York colleges he sought to study at: Columbia and Geneva (the latter now called Hobart and William Smith Colleges).

Smith instead began an apprenticeship to a blacksmith, but continued studying Greek and Latin. He did not abandon his dream of becoming a physician, and looked overseas to Scotland to continue his education. He was admitted to the University of Glasgow, which was abolitionist in sentiment and offered a medical education far superior to anything that could be found in the United States.

While in Scotland, Smith became a charter member of the Glasgow Emancipation Society. As a student, he completed bachelor's, master's, and medical degrees in five years, remaining at the top of his class the entire time. He thrived in a country where racism was not as endemic as in the United States, but did return to America in 1837.

He began practicing medicine, treating both Black and white patients from his office on West Broadway in Lower Manhattan. He also opened the first Black-owned pharmacy. Although he was never admitted to the American Medical Association, likely because of his race, he used his medical and scientific knowledge to write many articles that refuted racist claims about the intellectual capacities of people of color. The pseudoscience of phrenology was widely used in America at the time to denigrate the intellectual capabilities of Blacks and to help justify the system of slavery.

In addition to his medical and pharmaceutical practice, Smith also was the doctor for the Colored Orphan Asylum, a facility that housed six hundred to eight hundred children at any given time. In the four-day rampage of brutal violence known as the New York City Draft Riots in July 1863, a mob that included women and children broke into the asylum, stole everything they could get their hands on, and set fire to the building.

The riots began in protest to the unequal manner in which men were conscripted into military service for the Civil War. In addition, the rioters—many of whom were Irish immigrants and their descendants—targeted Blacks with violence because they feared a flood of freed slaves to Northern states would diminish their own chances of holding on to decent jobs. Indeed, some employers in this time period had used Black workers as strikebreakers.

The Colored Orphan Asylum was targeted on July 13, 1863, the first day of rioting. The July 25 minutes of the board overseeing the institution noted, "On the 13th July at 4 p.m., an infuriated mob . . . surrounded the premises of the Asylum and 500 of them entered the house . . . they deliberately set fire to it . . . simply because it was the home of unoffending colored orphan children."

Although the children housed at the asylum did escape to safety on Blackwell's Island (now Roosevelt Island), one hundred residents of color were killed and more than $1.5 million of property damage was caused (the equivalent of approximately $38 million today). Many members of the Black community fled Manhattan during or shortly after the violence and did not return. Smith himself moved his family and medical practice to Brooklyn.

Smith married Malvina Barnet in the 1840s. She was the daughter of a New York family of high social standing. Both husband and wife were of mixed racial background, and some of their surviving children would later pass for white. The couple had seven children, but three would die at a young age. His sons who survived married white women, while his daughter remained unmarried.

Smith and Douglass eventually broke with abolitionist William Lloyd Garrison, who believed that so-called "moral suasion" could lead to the end of slavery. Smith and others in his radical abolitionist faction, however, believed violence might be necessary to fight back against the powerful economic institution of slavery. Smith wrote in an 1856 essay, "Our white brethren cannot understand us unless we speak to them in their own language; they recognize only the philosophy of force."

Smith was a prominent speaker in abolitionist circles. In 1841, he spoke about the Haitian Revolution that resulted in the world's first Black republic. His speech focused on the brutal slavery that led to the uprising in the island nation, noting: "The slave system in this portion of the island, therefore, destroyed upwards of 5,000 human beings per annum."

The Black republic that resulted from the Haitian Revolution caused a deep-seated fear among slaveholders and others in America who benefited economically from the institution of slavery. Most industrialized nations, including the United States, refused to recognize Haiti as a nation, and used it—as well as Nat Turner's Rebellion in 1831—as justification for imposing stricter laws and regulations about the movements and actions of enslaved Blacks in America.

The Smiths also used the money they were fortunate enough to have earned in part to help other members of the Black community. For example, they donated a substantial amount of money to provide free farmland to Blacks in the New York community of Florence. The Florence Farming Association was the brainchild of activist Gerrit Smith, who established the community in 1848, and saw it as a means by which Blacks could gain suffrage, since New York law required them to own $250 worth of property in order to vote. Some ninety Black families took the opportunity to farm there, although the community dissolved by 1860.

Smith also was a prolific writer. In addition to essays and historic, political, and scientific articles, he wrote the introduction to Frederick Douglass's 1855 autobiography, *My Bondage and My Freedom*. When Douglass changed the name of his abolitionist newspaper *The North Star* to *Frederick Douglass' Paper*, Smith became his New York correspondent.

By the time of the Civil War, Smith was suffering from congestive heart failure, slowing down in many ways. Although he was appointed in 1863 as a professor at Wilberforce College, he was too sick and weak to accept the position. He died less than a month before slavery in America was officially ended with the ratification of the Thirteenth Amendment to the Constitution. James McCune Smith is buried in Cypress Hills Cemetery in Brooklyn, New York.

Rhode Island
Strong Social and Economic Ties to Slavery

In 1779, the desperate pleas of an enslaved South Kingstown woman, fearing she would soon be shipped to the South and separated from her young children, resulted in an unusual and early anti-slavery declaration from Rhode Island's government.

That year, a North Carolinian named John Rice showed up in Rhode Island on a spring day, seeking to purchase enslaved people. Carder Hazard of South Kingstown agreed to sell Rice an enslaved woman known only as Abigail and three of her daughters, who were seven years old and younger. After the transaction, Rice temporarily left Abigail with Hazard while he sought other enslaved humans to buy. When he returned to the Hazard farm to claim Abigail and her children, he hired two local men to help him transport his human property. Abigail pleaded with one of these hired men, Lodowick Stanton of Charlestown, to help her and her daughters stay in Rhode Island.

Stanton agreed. First, he offered to buy Abigail. When Rice refused to sell, Stanton, no doubt aided by others in the community, hid Abigail and her children for several weeks. The General Assembly in Rhode Island, likely at the urging of Stanton and others, got involved. The Assembly dealt harshly with Rice in the case because he had misrepresented himself as being from Hartford, Connecticut, instead of from a similarly named town in North Carolina. The Assembly ordered that Abigail and her children be sold back to someone local and kept in Rhode Island.

When Rice then sought financial relief for his loss, the General Assembly instead enacted legislation prohibiting the sale of enslaved people residing in Rhode Island to those who would take them out of state, unless the enslaved people in question approved of the move. The Assembly wrote: "Whereas tolerating Strangers to purchase Negroes, or Mulatto Slaves in this State, and carry them off either by Land or Water, against their consent, to perpetuate their Slavery in foreign Parts remote from the Friends and Acquaintance[s], is against the Rights of human Nature, and tends greatly to aggravate the Condition of Slavery, which this General Assembly is disposed to alleviate, till some favorable Occasion may offer its total Abolition."

While the ruling foreshadows an eventual end to slavery and, for the time period, offers an unusually sympathetic position on the hardships suffered by the enslaved, it is not an example of any universally held principles in Rhode Island. In fact, both the economy and the social fabric in Rhode Island in the colonial period, as well as in the years between the American Revolution and the Civil War, were more inextricably intertwined with the South than in most Northern states.

Both Providence and Warwick passed local laws as early as 1652 that limited the enslavement of both Africans and Native Americans. These local directives were largely ignored, however, and by 1703, Rhode Island codified the enslavement of both of these groups of people. Rhode Island—with its long seacoast from which merchant ships regularly set sail on trading missions to Africa and the West Indies, its sprawling farms in the part of the state now known as South County, and, later, its booming textile industry that used Southern cotton and supplied fabric to clothe Southern slaves—was a major player in the global slave trade. By the middle of the eighteenth century, it had the highest percentage of enslaved people in all New England.

The first enslaved people in Rhode Island, as in some other parts of New England, were Native Americans defeated during the Pequot and King Philip's wars. Rhode Islanders later turned to captured Africans to use as domestic servants, in numerous trades, and as farm laborers. The first enslaved Africans came to Rhode Island just after 1638, but by about 1750, some 10 percent of Rhode Islanders were enslaved.

During the years of the transatlantic slave trade, some 60 percent of the voyages from America originated from Rhode Island. It's estimated Rhode Island ships carried more than 100,000 Africans into slavery in the Americas, with about half of them illegally trafficked. Some of these enslaved people were transported back to Rhode Island and other American colonies and, later, states. Many others were brought to sugar plantations in the West Indies. Slavery resulted in vast fortunes for some Rhode Islanders, including the DeWolf family of Bristol, the largest slave-trading family in North America.

Some of Rhode Island's oldest and most respected institutions have deep ties to the slave trade. Brown University, founded in 1764 as the College of Rhode Island, counts a slave owner as its first president. Many of those who sat on its governing board also were slave owners. The Brown family for whom the university is now named were also involved in the slave trade.

A split between the Brown brothers over the morality of slavery also is well documented. Moses became a Quaker, a religious order that began turning against slavery in the 1700s. In 1760 in Newport, the Quakers adopted a resolution asking members to avoid business enterprises connected to promoting slavery, and further resolved that members who were slave owners should treat their human property with dignity and respect. By 1773, however, the Quakers took their directive a step further by threatening to expel from Quakerism any slave owner who did not immediately free their slaves.

Moses Brown freed his slaves at this time. According to an article titled "Slavery, the Slave Trade, and Brown University," part of Brown University's *Slavery and Justice Report*, Moses Brown read the following deed of manumission on November 10, 1773, with his family members present:

> *Whereas I am clearly convinced that the buying and selling of men of what color soever is contrary to the Divine Mind manifest in the conscience of all men however some may smother and neglect its*

reprovings, and being also made sensible that the holding of negroes in slavery however kindly treated has a tendency to encourage the iniquitous practice of importing them from their native country and is contrary to that justice, mercy, and humanity enjoined as the duty of every Christian, I do therefore by these presents for myself, my heirs, etc., manumit and set free the following negroes being all I am possessed of or any ways interested in.

By the Revolutionary era, Rhode Island lawmakers were starting to become much less accepting of the institution. Moses Brown helped draft a bill that was passed by the General Assembly in 1774, outlawing the direct importation of enslaved Africans into Rhode Island. A 1775 bill proposed a gradual abolition to slavery in the colony, but it was defeated.

Finally, in 1784 the state passed a gradual emancipation act that stipulated no child born after March 1, 1784, could be enslaved. In 1787, the state passed a law making it illegal for any Rhode Islander to be involved with the slave trade, even if they did not practice it within the state's boundaries.

In 1789, Moses Brown and others formed the Abolition Society in Rhode Island. But it would not be until 1843 that Rhode Island completely banned slavery. And the economic and social ties between Rhode Island and Southern slaveholders would continue to mean that a large proportion of Rhode Islanders supported slavery, as well as the pseudoscience spewed during the antebellum years to justify slavery. It contended that Blacks were intellectually inferior and that they were suited only for physical toil under white supervision.

In recent years, Rhode Island has taken many steps to recognize and deal with its historical ties to slavery. In 2003, Brown University began investigating its own ties to slavery, and in 2006 released its groundbreaking *Slavery and Justice Report* that confronted this unpleasant past. In 2012, it founded the Ruth J. Simmons Center for the Study of Slavery and Justice.

Other projects include the Newport Middle Passage Project that was established to commemorate and honor the thousands who died in the Middle Passage slave trade. Also, the Rhode Island Slave History Medallion project seeks to commemorate and mark with bronze medallions historic sites with links to slavery.

One statewide measure was taken in 2020. That year, Rhode Island voters dropped the phrase "and Providence Plantations," from the state's formal name because of the close connection the word *plantation* has to the institution of slavery.

George T. Downing
Newport Restaurateur and School Integrationist

George T. Downing and his family. (P5172, Collection of the Newport Historical Society / Courtesy of the Rhode Island Black Heritage Society)

When George Thomas Downing was just fourteen years old, he organized a literary society of his peers. The serious-minded young teenagers in the group discussed so-called "live subjects," and at one point adopted a resolution saying they would not celebrate the Fourth of July because they believed the Declaration of Independence was a mockery to people of color.

While his strong convictions about racial justice and equal rights began at an early age, throughout his life Downing demonstrated his beliefs through action. Receiving an invitation to be introduced to Millard Fillmore, for example, Downing politely refused, saying he would not shake the presidential hand that signed the Fugitive Slave Act of 1850, the law that allowed slave owners to legally reclaim their self-emancipated slaves even after those individuals were living in states where slavery was illegal. In 1841, Downing was beaten by railroad workers when he attempted to ride on the segregated Harlem Railroad in New York. During the Civil War, he agreed to help recruit Black soldiers for the Union Army only after receiving written assurances from authorities that the recruits would be treated equally and receive the same pay as their white compatriots. In addition, he tirelessly advocated for school integration in Newport, Rhode Island, a goal that was achieved after the Civil War.

Unlike many abolitionists, Downing did not see his work on behalf of people of color as complete following the passage of the Fifteenth Amendment to the Constitution, which granted voting rights to Black men. Instead, after its passage he turned his efforts toward advocating for fairer treatment for Black workers and equal rights for women of all races. In 1871, at a Colored National Labor Union Convention, Downing gave an address that included these thoughts: The "colored laborer in America has been the special victim of avarice and cupidity from the time he first set foot on the continent. . . . He has been held in abject slavery, despoiled of all rights, consequently is, as must be the case, extremely poor. He was freed from the claim of an individual master and became more completely a slave to the impoverished circumstances that environed him."

Downing, like his father before him, was a successful restaurateur in New York City. He later extended his restaurant and catering skills to Rhode Island, running a catering business in Providence. He took advantage of the burgeoning status of Newport as a summer resort for the wealthy in the mid-nineteenth century by building and operating the Sea-Girt House. Later, in Washington, DC, he oversaw the House of Representatives dining room for many years, a position that afforded him close associations with some of the country's leading lawmakers.

While Downing would enjoy financial success as an adult because of the popularity of his restaurants, his early life was more humble. He was born on December 30, 1819, in New York City. His grandparents were freed from slavery by the wealthy Virginia planter who owned them, and Downing's father Thomas was born free in 1791. John Downing, the planter, frequently entertained the elite of Virginia society, and Thomas grew up learning how to cater to the tastes of wealthy society, setting him on the road to success as a restaurateur.

Thomas Downing left Virginia for Philadelphia, where he married a free Black woman named Rebecca West. They moved to New York City, where Thomas opened an oyster house that served a wealthy business clientele and foreign visitors, including Charles Dickens. The couple had five children, of whom George was the oldest.

George Downing benefited from his parents' emphasis on education for their children. He attended a school on Orange Street in Manhattan, then the African Free School on Mulberry Street, where his classmates included many of the young men who would become the leading Black activists and abolitionists in the country. Downing continued his education at Hamilton College in his home state. In 1841, Downing married Serena Leanora de Grasse, and the couple went on to have ten children.

Following college, George Downing joined his father Thomas in the restaurant business and, probably more importantly, in his father's work assisting self-emancipating slaves safely on their road to freedom. Father and son were both active conductors on the Underground Railroad. A 1910 booklet titled "George Thomas Downing, Sketch of His Life and Times," by S. A. M. Washington, notes that Downing "inherited his father's commanding figure and kingly bearing, his aggressive temperament and manly character."

In 1846, George Downing moved to Newport to start his own oyster house restaurant. He also began a catering business in Providence, and by

1854, was back in Newport, constructing an impressive building called the Sea-Girt House on South Touro Street. This street is now part of the extremely fashionable Bellevue Avenue, location of many huge and stately summer "cottages" built by the wealthiest families in America. The Sea-Girt House encompassed a restaurant, a catering business, overnight accommodations for men, and the Downings' residence.

> GEO. T. DOWNING,
> OF NEW YORK,
> PROPRIETOR OF THE
> SEA-GIRT HOUSE,
> DOWNING'S BLOCK, SOUTH TOURO ST.
> FAMILY BOARDING-HOUSE.
> Confectionery, with French and other made dishes, sent out.

Advertisement for the Sea-Girt House, taken from the Newport City Directory (1858). (Public Domain / Courtesy of Rhode Island Historical Society)

In 1860, the Sea-Girt House was destroyed by a suspicious fire. Some sources say it was set by someone who did not appreciate Downing's activism on behalf of his race. Downing was undeterred by the setback, however, and rebuilt the Downing Block on the site. That building, which still stands, was the first block of stores focused on summer business in Newport.

In 1855, Downing began a blistering campaign calling for school desegregation in Newport. He repeatedly and persistently fought for educational equality, and frequently strategized with Massachusetts senator Charles Sumner about how the campaign should proceed. Downing argued that Blacks had fought heroically during the

Revolutionary War, and also had supported the Law and Order party that in 1841–1842 had opposed the Dorr Rebellion, which had advocated for an expansion of voting rights in Rhode Island. Although the Law and Order party opposed the rebellion, its members also rewrote the state constitution that did expand voting rights to many groups of men, including Black men.

In 1866, Downing's campaign to end school segregation finally succeeded when the state legislature ended the practice. Downing remained close to Sumner and was at his side when the senator died in 1874.

Downing also continued to be active in the Black Convention movement. In addition to ending school segregation, the movement supported more equal treatment of Black workers, along with better pay and working conditions. In 1869, Downing helped form the Colored National Labor Union.

From 1865 to 1877, Downing oversaw the dining room at the US House of Representatives. His position there gave him access to powerful lawmakers, and he lobbied them for laws aimed at expanding rights and opportunities for people of color. One such law opened access to public accommodations in Washington, DC, to Blacks. Downing worked to open the US Senate Gallery to Blacks, and he and his family were the first people of color to occupy box seats at a Washington, DC, theater.

In Rhode Island, Downing lobbied for an end to the state's law prohibiting interracial marriage. In Newport, he contributed a substantial amount of money that helped create Touro Park, and was part of a successful effort that extended Bellevue Avenue to Bailey's Beach. Although Downing was financially successful and considered one of the wealthiest and most influential Black men in Rhode Island, he failed at his attempts to gain elective office in Newport. In the 1880s, he ran unsuccessfully for a seat on the state's general assembly on three separate occasions.

Downing died in 1903 in Newport. Obituaries for him were published in many newspapers, including the *New York Times*, the *Boston*

Globe, and the *Cleveland Gazette*. The *Globe*'s obituary called him "the foremost colored man in the country." He was buried in Newport's Island Cemetery. A century after his death in 2003, Downing was inducted into the Rhode Island Heritage Hall of Fame for his work advocating for equal rights and treatment for people of color in the state.

George Fayerweather III
Blacksmith, Abolitionist, and Underground Railroad Conductor

On December 2, 1869, Prudence Crandall wrote a letter from her home in Illinois to longtime friend Sarah Harris Fayerweather in Kingston, Rhode Island. "I had not heard of the death of your dear husband till your letter came," she wrote, referencing George Fayerweather's death in November. "I feel that you are not without consolation in the midst of your bereavement. Your dear children are coming up so nobly to fill honorable positions in life; they must be a great comfort to you."

In addition to the personal message, Crandall also wrote about the national issues for which she and the Fayerweathers had worked for many decades. With the Civil War over and slavery ended throughout the country, Crandall wrote that she was happy to be alive to see that day arrive. She added: "I thank God that [William Lloyd] Garrison has lived to see the shackles fall from the slave."

Crandall and Harris Fayerweather had been friends for more than three decades at that point. The letter, with its combination of personal and political messages, well illustrates the lives they led right up to their deaths.

George Fayerweather and his wife were active in the fight to promote civil rights and equal opportunities for people of color and to end the institution of slavery. George Fayerweather was a conductor on the Underground Railroad; the couple hosted prominent abolitionists such as Frederick Douglass at their South Kingstown, Rhode Island, home; and, while living in Connecticut, George represented New London at the 1849 Colored Men's Convention in New Haven. That convention highlighted injustices suffered by people of color and called for the state to extend voting rights to Black men. This plea was ignored by state lawmakers, and Black men would not gain the vote in Connecticut until the state ratified the Fifteenth Amendment in 1870.

Sarah Harris and Prudence Crandall, and likely George Fayerweather, all met when they were living in eastern Connecticut in the 1830s, in or around the rural town of Canterbury, or in the nearby city of Norwich, with its active Black community. Harris was the first young Black woman to request admission to Crandall's school for girls, leading to Crandall's decision to remake her academy. When Crandall began admitting only girls of color, she touched off a shameful period of racism in Connecticut, as neighbors and lawmakers protested the school's existence, and ultimately passed the state's so-called Black Law, prohibiting students of color from being educated in Connecticut without prior local approval.

As Crandall's dream of running an acclaimed school for Black girls was falling apart in Canterbury, Harris and Fayerweather's life together was just beginning. In 1833, in a double-ring ceremony in Canterbury's Westminster Congregational Church, Sarah Harris married George Fayerweather, and Sarah's brother Charles married Mariah Davis, who worked for Prudence Crandall. Sarah Harris was twenty-one years old at the time of her marriage, while her husband was ten years older than she. In 1834, Harris and Fayerweather named their first child Prudence Crandall Fayerweather. She was born on the day Crandall's school was attacked by an angry, racist mob.

George, as did many in the reformer community, had close ties to the hated institution of slavery in the country. His grandfather, also named George, was enslaved by Reverend Samuel Fayerweather, who was the minister at St. Paul's Episcopal Church in Wickford, Rhode Island. When the elder George gained his freedom around 1770, he took his owner's surname, as was common among the formerly enslaved.

George's father, again, also named George, established a blacksmith shop in Kingston, a village that was called Little Rest at the time. In 1820, he built his home next to the forge. His son Solomon, and also his son George III, who was born in 1802, followed in his footsteps in that trade.

Members of the Black community in the nineteenth century and earlier were barred from the most prestigious and lucrative jobs due to racism. As such, many decided to become entrepreneurs, running small businesses of all types. In nineteenth-century America, the blacksmith was a vitally important craftsman in every community. Although today the trade is associated almost exclusively with shoeing horses, in the 1800s, blacksmiths made or repaired all types of metal tools. An account book for the Fayerweather forge, held in the University Archives and Special Collections at the University of Rhode Island, shows that the Fayerweathers made wheels, hooks, nails, and other tools, along with shoeing horses.

Blacksmiths generally were highly regarded, respected, and active in their communities. The Fayerweathers apparently were no different in this regard than others practicing the trade. At a time when racism ran deep in American society, such general community respect for a family of color was somewhat rare. The Fayerweathers combined the heritages of two marginalized communities—Black and Native American. George's mother was Nancy Rodman, who was descended from Narragansett sachem Ninigret I.

In the 1840s, Sarah and George Fayerweather moved to New London, Connecticut, a small city at the mouth of the Thames River whose economy relied heavily on whaling and other marine trades. He purchased a blacksmith shop that had been owned by B. S. Scoville. The couple lived just a short distance from the forge, and would eventually raise as many as nine children, although sources vary on exactly how many children the couple had. By 1850, they owned real estate valued at some $800.

Fayerweather's profession was vitally important during this time period in New London. The seacoast city was in the midst of an economic boom because of the whaling trade. New London was the second-busiest whaling port in the country, and the relatively short-lived business that fueled the burgeoning Industrial Revolution depended on a wide variety of metal tools.

In 1853, the family bought property in Kingston, Rhode Island. By 1855, George decided to move his family back to his home village. He joined his brother Solomon in running the family's blacksmith forge there, and George and Sarah and their family lived at the nearby Helme house. It was also in Kingston that the family assisted self-emancipating slaves on their way to freedom on the Underground Railroad, becoming more active in abolitionist causes and events. The Kingston village home was a center of abolitionist activity, meetings, and discussions, along with serving as lodging for abolitionist speakers coming to or through the area.

Long after slavery was abolished in the United States and George and Sarah had died, the Fayerweather family remained well-known and respected in southern Rhode Island. The small cottage George III's father had built in 1820 continued to be occupied by family members for more than 130 years. One of George and Sarah's granddaughters, Mrs. Arthur Perry, was the last family member to live in the house, which had become quite ramshackle by the 1950s. Mrs. Perry was an accomplished musician and a piano teacher. After her death, her husband remained in the house until he died in 1962.

In 1965, the Fayerweather house was bought by the Kingston Improvement Association. Dr. Carl Woodward, the retired president of the nearby University of Rhode Island, helped spearhead a fund-raising drive to restore the home. In 1966, the house became the new home of the Fayerweather Craft Guild, which continues to occupy the building, operating a gift shop there.

Remnants of the important lives of many generations of Fayerweathers remain at the site. Besides the display panels in the shop that tell some of the family's story, in the house's east room, the initials "GF," for George Fayerweather, can be seen on the floor. Just east of the house, the remains of the base of the once-thriving forge still exist. The restoration of the home also led to the discovery of many letters written between Prudence Crandall and Sarah Harris Fayerweather and the Fayerweather daughters. These were dated from 1869 to 1881.

George Fayerweather III was followed in death by his wife, in 1878. Both are buried, along with other family members, in South Kingstown's Old Fernwood Cemetery.

The Fayerweather House—now home to the Fayerweather Craft Guild, in Kingston village—is the site of the forge where the Fayerweathers worked. (Author's Collection)

Isaac Rice

Spurred to Activism by Firsthand Stories of Slavery's Horrors

Newport's long-standing inextricable economic and social ties with the South somewhat ironically led in the nineteenth century to the organization of both abolitionist groups and fierce anti-abolitionist sentiments among many city residents and leaders.

Southern visitors spent summers in Newport as early as the 1720s, and by the nineteenth century, when it was developing into the so-called Queen of Resorts, Southerners were some of the first to build elaborate summer homes in Newport. As such, the Southern elites were an integral part of the social fabric of Newport, even as Northern shipping and manufacturing was reliant on the Southern economy.

Southern slave owners also brought their human property with them to Aquidneck Island, where Newport is located, during the summer season, opening the door to a much darker side to Southern plantation life. The enslaved built relationships with members of Newport's free Black community, sharing many accounts of the atrocities of slavery, leading Newport's Blacks to agitate more strongly against the institution.

Isaac Rice, a successful businessman in Newport, was one Black leader who heard these stories and developed a deep hatred of the institution of slavery. This spurred him to activism and led him to become one of the city's most influential abolitionists and Black activists. His home at the corner of William and Thomas streets, just a block from the fashionable Bellevue Avenue, still stands today. A stop on the Underground Railroad, it was located in the Historic Hill section, one of several Black neighborhoods in Newport.

Rice was a member of the African Benevolent Society that established the first school to educate Black children in Newport. Rice also was a founding member of Newport's Colored Union Church and Society in 1824, a nondenominational house of worship specifically created for the city's community of color. He was also a distributor of the foremost abolitionist newspaper, *The Liberator*; a leader in the African Union Society; and a member of the Newport Anti-Slavery Society, serving as a delegate to state and national anti-slavery conventions. In 1843, the first year Black men were able to vote in Newport, Rice's name was added to the voter rolls.

Rice was born free in Narragansett, Rhode Island, in 1792 (or 1794, depending on the source). As a child, he was brought to Newport and spent most of the rest of his life there. He married Sarah Ann Conner Casey, and the couple had eight children. While it's especially difficult to get a true picture of historical figures' personalities and private lives, in the case of Rice, some letters written between he and Casey survive and remain in descendants' hands.

Family member Kimberly Dumpson wrote about some of these letters in a 2022 article for Rhode Island College, where she worked at that time as vice president of college advancement and external relations and director of the RIC Foundation. She wrote in the article:

> In 2020, I organized, digitized, and read the letters in chronological order. From this unique perspective, and as a loving and respectful onlooker, I peered into the authors' lives, their journeys, their struggles, and their love. As a parent, I was drawn to the letters written by my fourth-great-grandparents, abolitionists Isaac and Sarah Ann (Casey) Rice. I was moved by the love they shared for their children and their hopes and dreams for future generations. I felt anxiety from their struggles, pride in their accomplishments, and sorrow in their pain.

Because of the societal barriers that kept Blacks from entering many of the most lucrative and prestigious jobs available, Rice instead became an entrepreneur. He worked as a gardener for many years and became highly skilled at that trade. He was employed by many of Newport's most influential families, and while working for Rhode Island governor

William C. Gibbs, Rice planted the trees that still stand in Newport's Touro Park.

In addition to his work in landscaping, Rice also ran a catering business. Along with another prestigious Black restaurateur, George T. Downing, Rice in 1859 oversaw the food service at an August reunion for the sons and daughters of Newport.

According to an 1851 advertisement for George Pell's and Rice's catering and restaurant business in the *Newport Daily News*: "There may at all times be found there Oysters, game of all kinds, steaks, ham and eggs, puddings, pies and pastry of all kinds. Dinner will be served regularly to those who wish. In short, they intend to keep a first-class Refectory, and will guarantee to give satisfaction to all. Dinner and evening parties waited upon, and all delicacies and refreshments furnished, if desired."

Rice also made the acquaintance of future leading abolitionist Frederick Douglass when the latter was only recently self-emancipated. The two remained lifelong friends.

Despite the support for slavery among Newport's white business, social, and government leaders, anti-slavery sentiment also grew over time in the seaport city. In 1780, years before Rice was born, free Blacks in Newport founded the first mutual aid society for people of color in the United States. The Free African Union Society (FAUS) supported and financially assisted members of the Black community who were ill; who had suffered a death in the family; or who required help for other reasons. The group generally worked to bring the Black community together and condemned slavery, racism, and the slave trade.

In 1791, a year before Rice was born, the group in a written document denounced the slave trade and expressly cut ties with any member of the Black community linked to the trade. The document read, in part: "It [is] our indispensable duty not to associate ourselves [with] those who are of the African race that do, or hereafter be the means of bringing, from their Native Country, the Males, Females, Boys & Girls from Africa into bondage." The FAUS became the foundation of later anti-slavery, abolitionist, and civil rights groups and organizations in Newport, and paved the way for later organizations in which Rice would become a leader.

For example, Rice was a founding member of the Colored Union Church. According to information from the Newport Historical Society, the founding statement of the Union Church included the following: "We people of color of all denominations must come together to form one church; though we may differ in certain ways . . . we can agree on love and holding communion." The church's founding statement also indicated that a vital part of its mission was to uplift the children and others of color in Newport. The formation of the church constituted a statement of independence for the Black community, whose spiritual life previously was largely controlled by whites.

Abolitionists, anti-slavery reformers, and those seeking more equal rights for Blacks continued their work in Newport despite actions by white leaders that sought to quell these activities. In 1835, for example, a Newport town meeting passed a resolution full of blatant racial bigotry that was used to justify and support the institution of slavery. Further, the assembly supported a gag rule to prohibit abolitionist organizing and speeches and the dissemination of abolitionist newspapers and other literature.

While many members of Newport's Black community remained active in abolitionist causes throughout the 1830s and 1840s, by the 1850s some were expanding their activism to other areas. Rice, along with other Black Newporters such as George Downing, campaigned to desegregate Rhode Island schools. They sent petitions to the governor and state lawmakers. The sentiment of the majority white community, however, was communicated by the *Providence Journal*, which at the time contended that segregated schools were better for both white and Black students.

Public sentiment finally began to shift after the Civil War. More than one thousand Black Rhode Islanders served in the Union military forces during the war. The general public was grateful for this service that helped win the war. As such, there was a rethinking among some leaders about expanding civil rights for Blacks. In 1865, the Newport School Committee began allowing Black students to enroll in previously white-only schools, and in 1866, school integration was mandated throughout Rhode Island.

Rice died the same year school integration became the law in Rhode Island. He is buried in the Remington family plot in New Bedford, Massachusetts.

Isaac Rice House at 23 Thomas Street in Newport. (Author's Collection)

Vermont
First American Colonial Constitution to Prohibit Slavery

On July 8, 1777, the written constitution of the Free and Independent State of Vermont was adopted in Windsor, Vermont. The document outlawed slavery of men over the age of twenty-one and of women over the age of eighteen. In addition, the Vermont legislature granted voting rights to adult Black males. It was the first constitution in the American colonies to specifically prohibit slavery, a fact that has long been a point of deep pride among Vermonters.

The reality of slavery and Black subjugation in Vermont—along with the general treatment of Black residents by their white neighbors and the myth of an entirely slave-free Vermont—is much more complicated than that, however.

Jared Ross Hardesty, associate professor of history at Western Washington University, wrote a book titled *Black Lives, Native Lands, White Worlds; A History of Slavery in New England*. In an interview with Vermont Public in February 2020, Hardesty pointed out that despite the 1777 constitution's ban on slavery, legislation was passed in Vermont in the 1780s, and also in 1791, after it became the fourteenth US state, which indicates that enslaved people continued to live in Vermont, and that slave trading was still being practiced following the adoption of the Vermont constitution. According to Hardesty, laws during that time period banned slave trading and selling enslaved people outside of Vermont.

As it was in other New England colonies, slavery, in fact, was only gradually phased out in Vermont. Indentured servitude also was still allowed, and the white majority of Vermonters were not always welcoming to or accepting of free Black neighbors. Jeffrey Brace and his wife Susannah, for example, were harassed by their white neighbors in Poultney in the late eighteenth and early nineteenth centuries. They also were accused of being unfit parents, and Susannah's two children from a previous union were forced into indentured servitude because of this.

Andrew Harris also experienced intense cruelty in the state. Harris was a brilliant scholar who is recognized as the first Black graduate of the University of Vermont in 1838. Although admitted to study at the school, Harris endured almost complete social isolation while in Burlington, a situation that must have been particularly agonizing for a young man at a time in life when social interactions are central to one's well-being.

In Vermont, as elsewhere, even as the number of abolitionists was growing, abolitionism was not always embraced, and sometimes faced violent opposition. In Montpelier in 1832, for example, abolitionist Samuel May was driven off the stage as he attempted to deliver a speech.

The colonization movement also was popular in Vermont. Many colonizationists believed slavery should end, but also that racial integration would be intolerable. The movement instead advocated for resettlement of all Blacks to other countries, such as Liberia in Africa.

Vermont, as did other New England colonies, also often placed racist societal barriers that prevented Black residents from working specific types of jobs, obtaining higher education, owning land, and having complete freedom of movement. An article titled "Vermont 1777: Early Steps Against Slavery" by the National Museum of African American History and Culture also points out some general conditions that existed in New England: "If free blacks associated with slaves, both could and would be whipped. Anyone giving an African American a cup of hard cider was leveled with a heavy fine, whipped, or both."

Still, Vermont does have much to be proud of in terms of its Black history. It was a place where a Black minister led a nearly all-white congregation in West Rutland for some thirty years, beginning in the late 1700s. Lemuel Haynes, the Congregational minister, also was the first Black person to receive an honorary degree from an American college. He was granted an honorary master's degree in 1804 from Middlebury College.

In addition, Alexander Twilight was the first Black man to receive a bachelor's degree from an American college. He graduated from Middlebury College in 1823. Although it's now widely believed that because he was light-skinned, he likely often passed as white, Twilight was the first Black man to serve as a legislator, being elected to the state's House of Representatives in 1836.

In her book *Discovering Black Vermont*, Elise A. Guyette documents cooperation and mutual support between some of the earliest Black farmers and their white neighbors who settled in Hinesburg. "In these families we find not only the self-reliance and industry of Jefferson's yeoman farmer, but also cooperation and interdependence among the men and women in their biracial farming neighborhood." Farming on the Vermont frontier was difficult, at best, and neighbors often leaned heavily on one another for support.

Vermont also was home to many white residents who supported Blacks' efforts to end slavery, gain voting rights, and achieve a more equal footing with whites. The Vermont Anti-Slavery Society was formed in 1834. At its first meeting, one hundred delegates from thirty Vermont towns attended. By June of that year, individual towns throughout the state, including Peacham, Cabot, Barnet, and Danville, formed anti-slavery societies.

During the Civil War, some 166 Black Vermonters joined the Union forces. The state saw some 34,000 of all backgrounds serve.

Thaddeus Stevens, who represented Pennsylvania in Congress during the mid-nineteenth century, fought against racial discrimination and authored the Fourteenth Amendment, granting citizenship to all people born or naturalized in the United States, including the formerly enslaved. Stevens was born in Danville and spent his childhood in Vermont.

Members of the Robinson family of Ferrisburgh were radical abolitionists, and their home was a stop on the Underground Railroad. Their former home now operates as the Rokeby Museum.

Overall, the size of the Black population in Vermont was, and is, relatively small. Guyette's research revealed that the state's population was just 0.2 or 0.3 percent Black between 1790 and 1870. On the other hand, Vermont's total population was, and remains today, relatively small. Guyette points out that there were particular geographic locations in the state that had larger percentages of Black residents. In 1820, Burlington's population was 3.6 percent people of color, and in Hinesburg, where Guyette's research was focused on the early Black farmers who settled there, 2 percent of the population was Black.

Yet there has also been a kind of silence about any Black community's existence in Vermont, Guyette, writes noting the myth that Vermont was an entirely white state. "This erasure of people of color was bloodless violence, but violence nevertheless," she writes. Despite all of this, small Black communities did exist in Vermont in the nineteenth century, where Black residents achieved great things and left their mark on the state.

Rokeby Museum in Ferrisburgh is a National Historic Landmark. The Robinson family who lived there were abolitionists who sheltered self-emancipating slaves traveling to freedom on the Underground Railroad. (Author's Collection)

Jeffrey Brace
From Africa to Vermont

Icon created by artist Pamela Chatterton-Purdy and presented to the now-closed Green Mountain College in Poultney, where Brace once lived. (Courtesy of Pamela Chatterton-Purdy http://www.chatterton-purdyart.com/)

Jeffrey Brace has this to say about the misery of his life with one of a series of brutal masters who owned him in Connecticut in the mid-eighteenth century: "I have thought he took peculiar delight in whipping me, as I uniformly received about four whippings per day. If I was awkward, cried too much, or was lazy, it was sure to purchase me a good drubbing. Sometimes I got a flogging for freezing my feet while I was foddering and cutting the ice out of the watering place."

This is just one snippet from the many harrowing stories Brace recalls in his 1810 memoir, *The Blind African Slave*. As an elderly blind man living in northern Vermont, Brace narrated his story of hardship at the hands of a series of sadistic owners in America after he was snatched as a boy by slave catchers who were hunting humans in what is now Mali, Africa. If ever there is a story that soundly dispels the myth that slavery in the Northern colonies that became US states was more benign and humane than on Southern plantations, it is Brace's.

Despite the deprivations and physical brutality he suffered as an enslaved person, Brace fought nobly in both the French and Indian War and the American Revolution, became a Christian, learned to read, and finally, was granted his freedom. He became the first Black resident of the town of Poultney, Vermont. He joined a group of anti-slavery activists and spoke to groups about the horrors of living in slavery. He married, had children, and made a living farming. But even as a free man, he continued to suffer due to the racism of his neighbors, who harassed his family and sought to indenture his children. Near the end of his life, blind and destitute, he was forced to wage a three-year fight to secure the government pension that was owed him for his military service.

Although Brace's is one of just a handful of written narratives ever produced by enslaved people, it was largely forgotten for many decades, with only two known copies of it left in existence in contemporary times, one of which was in the special collections library at the University of Vermont. Even when the memoir was first published, Brace's story held little value for the radical abolitionists of the time because it focused on Northern slavery, where states had moved to end the practice. Nineteenth-century abolitionists focused their efforts on eliminating slavery in the South, where holding humans in bondage remained legal.

Kari J. Winter, a historian and professor of American Studies at the State University of New York at Buffalo, rediscovered Brace's story.

In an introduction written for a 2004 rerelease of Brace's memoir, she notes that the story was a mismatch for nineteenth-century abolitionist messaging.

But Brace's memoir, which he narrated to a young, white abolitionist lawyer named Benjamin F. Prentiss in St. Albans, Vermont, is certainly one that should be better known. Besides Brace's recollections of brutality at the hands of his enslavers, he also recalls the kindness of one woman who held him in bondage; his actions and wounds suffered in military service; his everyday life as a Vermont farmer; and the heartbreak of his wife's death. Even more important, his memoir takes readers inside the brutal depravity of the Middle Passage and back to Africa, where Brace was snatched as a teenager.

Jeffrey Brace was born Boyrereau Brinch around 1742 to a family of some prestige in a region of Africa that is likely in the southern part of the contemporary country of Mali. Brace calls his ancestral home the kingdom of Bow-woo. Around 1758, he was enjoying swimming with a group of friends when he was captured by slave hunters.

Brace recalls the day in his memoir:

Eleven out of fourteen were made captives, bound instantly, and notwithstanding our unintelligible entreaties, cries & lamentations, were hurried to their boat, and within five minutes were on board, gagged, and carried down the stream like a sluice; fastened down in the boat with cramped jaws, added to a horrid stench occasioned by filth and stinking fish; while all were groaning, crying and praying, but poor creatures, to no effect.

Aboard a ship bound for the British colony of Barbados, Brace estimates there were some three hundred captives. Conditions were deplorable. The captured Africans were given little food or water, and the crew members forced some of the female captives into sexual slavery. Once on the island of Barbados, life didn't improve for the Africans. Brace recalls the frequent beatings and general deprivation designed to subjugate the African captives and turn them into submissive laborers. One particularly gruesome story Brace recalls focuses on watching as a young African woman was beaten to death by her enslavers while her young brother watched and screamed. Throughout the memoir, Brace bluntly points out the hypocrisy of so-called Christian captors who displayed no mercy or humanity in their treatment of the captives.

Around 1760, Brace was sold to Captain Isaac Mills. Mills made Brace a soldier/sailor in service to the British during the Seven Years War, also called the French and Indian War. During one battle with a Spanish ship, Brace recounts that he was wounded several times. The most serious wound was caused by a musket ball that lodged in his right hip.

Brace continued in service to Mills, traveling with him to Dublin, Ireland; Savannah, Georgia; New York City; Newport, Rhode Island; Boston; and Halifax, Nova Scotia, before finally arriving in New Haven, Connecticut, in 1763. There, Mills sold Brace to John Burwell of the coastal town of Milford. Burwell was the first of several sadistic enslavers Brace endured in Connecticut.

He recounts about another: "I was sold to one Peter Pridon [Peter Prudden], son of the old priest Pridon, of Old Milford. I lived with him about two months and got five severe whippings for crying nights. From Pridon, I was bartered away for some old horses to one Gibbs." Brace had one more cruel owner before being sold to a widow named Mary Stiles, who lived in Woodbury, Connecticut. "This was a glorious era in my life, as widow Stiles was one of the finest women in the world; she possessed every Christian virtue," he recalls in the memoir.

Stiles treated Brace humanely and, most important, taught him to read and helped him improve his ability to communicate in English. When she died, he was passed down as property to her two sons. When their sons left to fight in the Revolutionary War, Brace also went to fight, recounting, "Poor African slave; to liberate freemen, my tyrants." This military service earned him his manumission, however. As a free man, Brace decided to head to the new state of Vermont, which had abolished slavery as part of its constitution.

Already more than forty years old by this time, Brace bought and cleared land in the wilderness of Poultney, Vermont, and married an African-born widow named Susannah Dublin. She entered the marriage with two children, and the Braces went on to have three more children together, as well.

Despite their free status, life was hardly easy for the Braces. Clearing and farming the rocky hillsides of Vermont was backbreaking, never-ending work. In addition, the couple faced the racism of their neighbors, who frequently harassed the family by tapping maple trees on the Braces' property and letting their cattle loose on Brace land. Their neighbors also accused the Braces of being unfit parents, and local authorities forced Susannah's two children into indentured servitude.

In 1802, after living more than fifteen years in Poultney and seeing that his own children also risked being forced into servitude, Jeffrey Brace moved the family farther north, to the town of Sheldon, Vermont. There, he was baptized and joined the Baptist Church in Georgia, Vermont, in 1805, indicating the couple had moved again. Just two years later, Susannah died.

Sometime after this, Brace began traveling throughout Vermont with a Baptist preacher named Charles Bowles. Brace recounted his harrowing stories of life in slavery to numerous audiences to help promote the anti-slavery cause, before he was encouraged to work with the abolitionist Benjamin Prentiss to complete the memoir.

At the end of his book, Brace recounts:

And now after having passed through so many varying scenes of life, and having lost my beloved companion, as before mentioned, and being left as it were, alone in this world, I have concluded it my duty to myself, to all Africans who can read, to the Church, in short to all mankind, to thus publish these memoirs, that all may see how poor Africans have been and perhaps now are abused by a Christian and enlightened people. Being old and blind, almost destitute of property, it may bring me something to make me comfortable in my declining days, but above all, it is my anxious wish that this simple narrative may be the means of opening the hearts of those who hold slaves and move them to consent to give them that freedom which they themselves enjoy, and which all mankind have an equal right to possess.

Unfortunately, as historian Kari Winter writes in the introduction to Brace's memoir, the book never sold many copies, so Brace likely did not receive the financial compensation he needed. However, he did receive, after a three-year struggle, enough money from a military pension to live out his days in Vermont. When he died on April 20, 1827, he was memorialized in a long obituary printed in a Poultney newspaper.

Although his story was then forgotten for more than a century, after it was rediscovered, numerous steps were taken to honor him. The University of Vermont, for example, awards book scholarships in Brace's name to students who demonstrate academic excellence and a commitment to social justice. Also, in 2008, a historical marker honoring Brace was unveiled in Poultney. More than sixty of his descendants attended the event.

Andrew Harris
Brilliant Orator, Shunned at the University of Vermont

On May 7, 1839, Andrew Harris addressed the crowd at the annual meeting of the American Anti-Slavery Society. He was scheduled to speak in a prominent time slot on the first morning of the convention. Just twenty-five years old at the time, his eloquent speech addressing, among other topics, the horrors of slavery, was published verbatim in the abolitionist newspaper *The Liberator* on May 16:

> *If the groans and sighs of the victims of slavery could be collected, and thrown out here in one volley, these walls would tremble, these pillars would be removed from their foundations, and we should find ourselves buried in the ruins of the edifice. . . . If the blood of the innocent, which has been shed by slavery, could be poured out here, this audience might swim in it,—or, if they could not swim they would be drowned. If the tears that slavery has caused to be shed were poured out here, there might be a sea on which to ply the oar in exercise of sport and diversion.*

Harris, who was a resident of Philadelphia by the time of this 1839 meeting, was by all accounts a gifted and eloquent orator. With a college degree, he was among the most educated of American Blacks at the time.

Despite the status he was gaining in the abolitionist, Black activist community, his path to the convention had not been a smooth one. He overcame many challenges in his pursuit of an education and career as a minister. While his oratory prowess might have rivaled that of Frederick Douglass, had he lived longer, instead Harris's life was cut short, just two years after he delivered the 1839 speech. With his potential never fully realized, Harris was all but forgotten for many decades.

Much later, he would be posthumously recognized by the University of Vermont, where he earned a college degree after being rejected for admittance to other colleges because of his skin color. Despite his admission to and graduation from UVM, he also was never embraced by the college community there.

Harris is the first Black graduate of the University of Vermont, and he joined a tiny group of Black American college graduates when he finished his studies in 1838. The Vermont Division of Historic Preservation and the university commemorated his achievement with an informational sign in 2015. Even then, however, it appeared that Harris was not fully embraced by the university, as the original placement of the sign was in a low-traffic area. In 2018, the sign was moved to a more prominent location on campus, a marble monument was added in his honor, and the university commons was renamed in recognition of Harris.

According to an article by R. J. Morrison in the independent university newspaper, *The Vermont Cynic*, published on February 6, 2022, the location change of the Harris sign occurred several months after Kevin P. Thornton—a Vermont resident who lectured in history at UVM and has researched and written about Harris—had a second article about Harris published by the Vermont Historical Society.

Harris was born in 1814 in New York State. While little is known about his earliest childhood, it's likely both of his parents were Black, as Thornton points out in his writings that the only physical description ever written about Harris described him as a "full-blooded Negro." His mother could have been as young as twelve years old when she became pregnant.

By the age of two, Harris became part of a white family headed by a Presbyterian minister in Cayuga, New York. He undoubtedly was influenced by the religious revivalism of the Second Great Awakening, stemming from both the family in which he was raised and the geographic area of his formative years. Parts of central and western New York became known as the "burned-over district" during this time period because the fervor of religious revivalism in the area was said to have spread like a forest fire.

Harris was intellectually gifted from a young age and attended the Geneva Lyceum, a college preparatory–type school attended by many who intended to enter the ministry. There, he learned Greek and Latin. When he was about twenty years old, he became fixed on attending college, a feat that was not easy for a Black man in America in the early nineteenth century.

His first choice was apparently Union College in Schenectady, New York. According to information in his obituary, he was rejected because college officials were wary of increasing abolitionist sentiment, as well as the racism that was touching off violence, such as the racist-motivated riots that occurred in July 1834 in New York City.

Harris then crossed the eastern boundary of New York to seek admission to Middlebury College in Vermont. He was again rejected because of his race. Traveling farther north, he turned to the University of Vermont, where he was admitted, although somewhat begrudgingly. The president of UVM at the time was Reverend John Wheeler, a devoted colonizationist. The colonization movement advocated for Blacks in America to be relocated to Africa. While Wheeler was no champion of equal rights for Blacks, Harris was a qualified candidate for admission who intended to make the ministry his life's work, and so, Wheeler accepted him to UVM.

UVM was a tiny, isolated, and struggling college at the time. It had just five faculty members and a very small number of students. Yet Harris, who entered UVM as a sophomore, was never embraced by his classmates. They were against his admission, and later threatened to boycott graduation ceremonies if Harris was allowed to deliver an oratory along with all the other graduates, as was the custom at the time.

Harris likely endured a lonely existence in Vermont. He was never listed in the catalog of students while he was there. His name was frequently listed last, while all other students were listed in alphabetical order on exam records. He was not allowed to attend college prayers and recitations with other students. In 1842, the *National Anti-Slavery Standard* wrote this about Harris and UVM: "Mr. Andrew Harris, unable to obtain a regular standing at Union College, went to the University of

Vermont; but even there, although allowed more privileges, he was not suffered to stand on the same footing with the other students."

Kevin Thornton agreed. In his article, "Postscript: Andrew Harris at the University of Vermont," published by Vermont History, he wrote: "To sum up, it appears that Harris was expected to be a silent presence in class, as well as invisible when it came to any public event."

Understandably, Harris left Vermont quickly after graduating in 1838. He headed briefly to Troy, New York, and then to New York City, with its much larger community of Black abolitionists and reformers. He was introduced to and made connections with some of the most influential Black reformers of the time before again moving on, this time to Philadelphia.

It was in that city that Harris came into his own, becoming an activist, sought-after speaker, and, ultimately, a pastor of the Black Presbyterian church on St. Mary Street. His ideas were considered radical. He not only called for an end to slavery, but also equality among the races, advocating for the use of politics to achieve these goals. In 1840, Harris was among the founding members of a new organization called the American and Foreign Anti-Slavery Society. He also helped form the Liberty Party, an abolitionist political party that ran candidates for the presidency in 1840 and 1844. Harris would not live to see the 1844 campaign, however. He died of a fever on December 1, 1841.

While Harris's life and accomplishments faded into obscurity for many years after his death, the words he spoke at the 1839 American Anti-Slavery Society, more recently rediscovered, seem today both ahead of his time and as remarkable as those of more well-known Black activists such as W. E. B. Du Bois, Frederick Douglass, and even Reverend Martin Luther King Jr.:

Again, in the social relations of life, wrongs are inflicted upon us that are grievous and heavy to be borne, and we must fold our arms and bear it. But even this is thrown out as a taunt against us, that we do not speak of our wrongs, as evidence that we are too stupid and degraded to feel them; while, if we rise to defend ourselves, and to plead our cause, the torch and the brick-bat are poured out as arguments on the other side.

Despite these challenges, Harris ended his speech with a fierce rebuke against the concept of colonization, concluding, "And while I live, let my prayer be, that the same soil which cherished my father may cherish me; and when I die, that the same dust may cover me that covered the ashes of my father."

Andrew Harris Commons and the historic marker commemorating Harris at the University of Vermont, Burlington. (Photo by Cara MacDonald, Cara Mac Media)

Lemuel Haynes

Pastor to White Congregation in West Rutland for Three Decades

Lemuel Haynes earned numerous firsts in his lifetime. He is likely the first Black man ordained as a Protestant minister in America. He is the first Black man to obtain an honorary master's degree in America, from Middlebury College in Vermont, in 1804. He also is likely the first Black minister in America to lead an all-white congregation, and wrote one of the earliest essays condemning the evils of slavery in the American colonies.

He was an eloquent speaker and preacher, a poet, intellectual, writer, patriot, husband, and father who was respected and admired in his lifetime. He also was among the earliest Black anti-slavery activists in America. His achievements are even more remarkable given his humblest and saddest of beginnings.

He penned one of his boldest and most forward-thinking of writings in 1776. While some sources say it was published or preached at that time, others indicate it wasn't discovered until some 150 years later. Titled "Liberty Further Extended: Or Free Thoughts on the Illegality of Slave-Keeping," it used words from the Declaration of Independence as the foundation upon which to build an argument against slavery.

Liberty is God-given, Haynes said in the essay. He wrote: "And the main proposition, which I intend for some Brief illustration is this, Namely, That an African, or in other terms, that a Negro may Justly Challenge, and has an undeniable right to his Liberty: consequently, the practice of Slave-keeping, which so much abounds in this Land is illicit."

Further into the essay, he wrote: "Therefore, we may reasonably Conclude, that Liberty is Equally as precious to a Black man, as it is to a white one, and Bondage Equally as intolerable to the one as it is to the other: Seeing it Effects the Laws of nature Equally as much in the one as it Does in the other."

Haynes was born to a white mother and Black father in 1753 in West Hartford, Connecticut. Little is known about his parents, and scholars have various theories about his mother; she could have been a white servant, or she might have been a woman from a more prominent family. What is known for sure is that Haynes was abandoned by both parents when he was still an infant, and became indentured until the age of twenty-one to Deacon David Rose and his family in Granville, Massachusetts, a town just north of the Connecticut border.

Marker commemorating the life of Lemuel Haynes, located in West Hartford, Connecticut. (Author's Collection)

Haynes actually recalled his time with the Rose family fondly, saying he was well cared for by Deacon Rose's wife, who apparently loved and doted on the boy. When he was old enough, Haynes helped with farmwork and spent time at church in the evenings. The family had a tradition of reading religious sermons, and one night, Haynes read one he had written himself. The family asked who the author was, and when Haynes said it was his own, it elicited praise and excitement.

Haynes did not have much formal education as a child, choosing to pursue the ministry as a way to secure both an education and a career. He was a voracious reader, and especially interested in reading the Bible and books on theology. Throughout his adolescence, he wrote his own sermons, reading them and conducting religious services locally, according to a biography of him posted on the PBS website as part of the television series *Africans in America*.

When Haynes's indenture ended in 1774, he was sufficiently swept up in patriotic fervor to enlist in the local militia. He was stationed at Fort Ticonderoga and responded to the Lexington alarm as part of the militia. It's likely that while he was encamped in Cambridge, he wrote a poem about the Battle of Lexington that also speaks to slavery. While the slavery mentioned in the poem appears to refer to the American colonists living as "slaves" to British tyrants, it could also be read as referring to the Black slavery that was legal in American colonies.

The poem reads, in part:

For Liberty, each Freeman Strives, as it's a Gift of God.
And for it willing yield their Lives and Seal it with their Blood.
Thrice happy they who thus resign into the peaceful Grave.
Much better there, in Death Confin'd, than a surviving slave.

Following the Revolution, Haynes returned to his pursuit of a career as a minister. He turned down an opportunity to attend Dartmouth College to instead study Latin and Greek with two ministers of note in Connecticut. In November 1780, he was licensed to preach, and was officially ordained as a Congregational minister in 1785. He remained in Granville for two more years, and married a white schoolteacher named Elizabeth Babbitt. The couple eventually had ten children.

Following his ordination, he first became pastor of an all-white congregation in Torrington, Connecticut, but left after two years due to tensions among some members of the congregation who objected to his race. He then moved to a predominantly white parish in West Rutland, Vermont, where he remained as pastor for thirty-one years.

He became known for his wit outside of church and his seriousness of purpose while preaching. The congregation expanded during his time in West Rutland, from forty-six members to more than three hundred, according to Mark Bushnell, a Vermont historian who wrote an article about Haynes for *VTDigger* in 2019. Bushnell wrote that Haynes became well known throughout a wide region, and was often invited to be a visiting preacher in other congregations. According to Bushnell, one fellow minister said of Haynes: "His enunciation, though remarkably clear, was extremely rapid; a delightful flow of words and thoughts, as if they were crowding each other for utterance."

In 1818, Haynes resigned from his position in West Rutland. Again, there's disagreement among those who have studied Haynes about what prompted it. Haynes was a federalist, and his more conservative views could have been the root of why he parted with the congregation. Haynes was also supposed to have told others the separation was due to his race and objections to it by some congregants.

Haynes moved to another congregation in Manchester, Vermont. After being there for three years, he moved to his final assignment in South Granville, New York, located just west of the Vermont border. He stayed there for eleven years.

Haynes died at the age of eighty on September 28, 1833. Haynes's prominence in his lifetime led to a biography being written about him in the 1830s, an extraordinary feat for a Black man in that era. Then, however, his life was largely forgotten. It's only in recent years that his accomplishments and his writings have been rediscovered and recognized for their immense significance.

Louden Langley
Advocate for Black Civil War Soldiers

On April 27, 1854, a letter lambasting the colonization movement was published in the *Green-Mountain Freeman*. It was written by a young Vermont native named Louden Langley, whose family was among the earliest Black settlers in Vermont. (Louden's name is spelled as "Loudon" in some articles and books.) His letter was frank in its disdain for the movement, promoted by a sizable number of whites, and popular in Vermont for some fifty years, which advocated for relocating American Blacks to other countries, including places in Africa:

> *If the Society is actuated with such a love for my people, let men so interested, and every other, cease their efforts in behalf of that society—for their labor is in vain, so far as regards to the triumph of their policy—and lend their influence in favor of giving us "liberty and equal rights" in the land of our birth.*

While advocating for fair treatment and equal rights may be mainstream today, in Langley's time, his words were considered radical. Langley became known for his strong opinions about equal rights for people of color, as well as his willingness to put his thoughts in writing for publication. He was a prolific writer of letters that were published in numerous newspapers in the nineteenth century. Besides writing against the colonization movement, he also wrote about the unfair treatment of Black soldiers serving for the Union during the Civil War, the need for equal rights for people of color, and the horrors of slavery. In his writing, he also said rebelling against unjust laws was an appropriate action.

Another letter he wrote to a newspaper in 1854 said this in regards to slavery: "I am no advocate of war, I mean an unjust war; and as bad as

I hate war, I hate tyrants and tyranny worse. . . . Yes, I go further, and I say that every nation has a God-given right to rebel against any laws, unjust laws, that the tyrants may deem fit to make and enforce."

Louden Langley was born in 1836 and grew up in rural northern Vermont, enjoying the support of an extended family that included his grandparents. It was unusual in this time period for people of color to have the opportunity to live closely together, in a compound of sorts. His family was among the earliest of Black settlers who, through backbreaking toil, cleared land for farming on a hill in Hinesburg, a Green Mountain community located just east of Lake Champlain and south of Burlington.

Langley and his brothers attended school in the integrated public district schoolhouse nearest their home. As Elise A. Guyette writes in her book *Discovering Black Vermont*, "The thirty-six to thirty-eight students attending the small school along with the Langley boys were from families representing the entire social spectrum of Huntington (a town adjacent to Hinesburg) at the time, from the small farmers to the richest in town. . . . Late in the century we see the outstanding results of this education in the Langleys' youngest son, Loudon."

In the 1850s, Langley's writing makes it clear that his family was among those who sheltered fugitive slaves in the immediate antebellum period. Guyette notes in her book that the practice might have begun even earlier, because by 1842, two men of color from Maryland were noted on grand lists from the neighborhood where the Langleys farmed. A letter by Langley published on February 8, 1855, in the *Green-Mountain Freeman* directly references a fugitive slave from Cuba whom Langley sheltered.

By the end of the 1850s, Langley had moved away from his family's farm. In 1859, he married a woman named Jane Anthony in Winooski Falls, Vermont.

In December 1863, Langley left his home state to fight for the Union in the Civil War. He originally strove to join the 1st South Carolina Volunteers, but due to an administrative error, he was instead assigned to the 54th Massachusetts Infantry Regiment, according to information from the National Park Service. The regiment was immortalized in the

1989 movie *Glory*, and is honored with a large monument and relief sculpture by Augustus Saint-Gaudens, located on Boston Common.

In June 1863, the regiment arrived in Beaufort, South Carolina, which was under Union control. The first military action the regiment saw was a skirmish on James Island on July 16, 1863. Just two days later, they led an attack on Battery Wagner, key to the assault on Charleston. It was a brutal fight, and in the end, more than 270 of the 650 soldiers fighting were killed, wounded, captured, or missing and presumed dead, according to information from the National Park Service.

Harriet Tubman, who witnessed the fighting, wrote of the battle: "And then we saw the lightening [*sic*], and that was the guns; and then we heard the thunder, and that was the big guns; and then we heard the rain falling, and that was the drops of blood falling; and when we came to get in the crops, it was the dead that we reaped."

Despite the losses, the regiment's performance in battle earned them high praise and support from military officials, including General Ulysses S. Grant.

Langley and his fellow soldiers, however, experienced unfair and unequal treatment in the military because of the color of their skin. Langley was not shy about speaking out against it. In the spring of 1864, he wrote a letter to the governor of Vermont, complaining of the unequal pay received by Black and white soldiers. While white soldiers were paid $13 a month and an additional $3.50 clothing allowance, Black soldiers received only $10 a month, with $3 deducted for clothing, according to a 1999 article in *Vermont History* that reprinted several of Langley's letters.

In a letter Langley wrote on January 23, 1864, to the *Weekly Anglo-African* in New York, he said, "Nine-tenths of the boys had been informed by the selectmen, who were very anxious to fill their town quotas, that the colored recruits received from the U.S. the same pay and bounty as the white recruits. The writer had warned and told all those who had been thus informed, that such was not the case; but the boys preferred to believe the misrepresentations with which the officers (either from ignorance or a love of falsehood), had filled their ears."

In the summer of 1864, pay was made equal between Black and white recruits. A May 21, 2015, article about Langley, published in

The Island Packet newspaper, reported that some historians directly link Langley's efforts to the governmental action to equalize pay.

Despite his dissatisfaction with unequal pay and treatment, Langley remained in the military until 1866, rising to the rank of sergeant major. He also apparently grew to enjoy South Carolina, or believed he could effect more positive changes there, so by the time he mustered out, he decided to not return to Vermont. He instead stayed in Beaufort County, settling there with his wife and four children.

The end of slavery and the Civil War did not end Langley's activism. He became involved with Reconstruction-era politics, and in the 1868 South Carolina Constitutional Convention, represented Beaufort County, along with famous Black politician and leader Robert Smalls, who later was elected to the US House of Representatives. During the convention, Langley advocated for free and equal education, and later served as a school commissioner for Beaufort County.

Unfortunately, as whites in the South began to use force and violence to reassert their authority and power, most Blacks were again voted out of office. Langley began working as an assistant keeper of the Hunting Island Lighthouse near Beaufort. *The Island Packet* article notes that by this time, Langley likely was plagued by a back injury he had suffered during the war, which led to other health problems.

He was just forty-three years old when he died on June 28, 1881. He is buried in Beaufort National Cemetery, far from his native Vermont, but close to many others who believed deeply in the promise of an end to slavery and equal rights for Blacks.

Hunting Island Lighthouse. (South Carolina State Parks)

Louden Langley's grave at Beaufort National Cemetery in South Carolina. (Courtesy of James D. Ballard, cemetery administrative specialist, Beaufort National Cemetery)

Bibliography

Connecticut

"Abolitionist Dwight P. Janes: A Real New London Hero of the *Amistad*." New London Maritime Society, August 23, 2014.
"*Amistad* Case." National Archives, https://www.archives.gov/education/lessons/amistad.
"Connecticut Abolitionists." National Park Service, nps.gov.
"Early Anti-Slavery Advocates in 18th Century Connecticut." *Connecticut History*, connecticuthistory.org, CT Humanities.
Farrow, Anne, Jenifer Frank, and Joel Lang. *Complicity: How the North Promoted, Prolonged and Profited from Slavery*. New York: Ballantine Books, 2005.
"History of Slavery in Connecticut." Wikipedia entry.
Normen, Elizabeth J., ed. *African American Connecticut Explored*. Middletown, CT: Wesleyan University Press, 2013.
Plummer, Dale. "Norwich's Ties with the Underground Railroad." *Norwich* magazine, February 2013.
"Slavery and Abolition: Connecticut History." *Connecticut History*, connecticuthistory.org, CT Humanities.
Williams, Donald E., Jr. *Prudence Crandall's Legacy: The Fight for Equality in the 1830s, Dred Scott, and* Brown v. Board of Education. Middletown, CT: Wesleyan University Press, 2014.

Jehiel C. Beman

"Abolition, Colonization and the Underground Railroad." Cross Street A.M.E. Zion Church: Struggle, Jubilee, Vision, Wesleyan University website.
"African Americans in Middletown." Cross Street A.M.E. Zion Church, Wesleyan University website.
Baskauf, Carmen, and Lucy Nalpathanchil. "Acknowledging Middletown's Ties to Slavery." *Snap Judgment*, Connecticut Public Radio, October 24, 2019.
Beman, Jehiel C. Letter to Frederick Douglass, September 7, 1854, The Frederick Douglass Papers Project website.
"Beman Triangle." Wesleyan University website.
Dunavin, Davis. "Be(a)man." WSHU, April 3, 2020.
"History of the Beman Triangle." Office of Residential Life, Wesleyan University website.
Housley, Kathleen. "Yours for the Oppressed: The Life of Jehiel C. Beman." *Journal of Negro History*, Winter 1992.

James, Jennifer Lee. "Jehiel C. Beman: A Leader of the Northern Free Black Community." *Journal of Negro History*, Winter 1997.
"Jehiel Beman, Community Leader." Cross Street A.M.E. Zion Church, Wesleyan University website.
Maune, Bill. "UNESCO Unveiling of the Plaque in Middletown." Patch.com, September 29, 2019.
Nasta, Jesse. "Middletown's Beman Triangle: A Testament to Black Freedom and Resilience." *Connecticut History*, connecticuthistory.org, CT Humanities, December 13, 2023.
———. "Talking About Preservation: Middletown's Beman Triangle." Video of live presentation, May 15, 2024, https://www.youtube.com/watch?v=p60vGRglVpM.
Slattery, Brian. "Doc Reveals the New Haven HBCU that Could Have Been." *New Haven Independent*, February 23, 2023.
Stannard, Ed. "Slavery in Connecticut, Ended Only in 1848, Had a Long History." *Middletown Press*, June 19, 2020.

Sarah Harris Fayerweather

"African Americans in Kansas." Wikipedia entry.
Alexander, Shawn Leigh. "A Brief History of Race Relations in Kansas." American Civil Liberties Union website.
Clark, Emily. "Sarah Harris Fayerweather." *Connecticut History*, connecticuthistory.org, CT Humanities, June 10, 2024.
DiMartino, Joanie. "Historically Speaking: Harris Sisters Linked to Prudence Crandall's Canterbury School." *Norwich Bulletin*, March 14, 2021.
Fayerweather Family Papers. University of Rhode Island Library, University Archives and Special Collections.
"Harris Sisters Month." Otis Library website, Norwich, Connecticut.
"(H)our History Lesson: Prudence Crandall, Sarah Harris, and a Struggle for Black Women's Education." National Park Service, nps.gov.
Kansas African American History Trail. Kansas African American Museum, tkaahistorytrail.org.
Kansas Museum of History Tours. Kansas Historical Society, kansashistory.gov.
Menders, Julie, and Elanah Sherman. "Historically Speaking: Otis Library Celebrates Lives of Harris Sisters This Month." *Norwich Bulletin*, April 4, 2021.
National Register of Historic Places. Application, Jail Hill, Norwich, March 8, 1999.
Plummer, Dale, Norwich City Historian. Interview, June 30, 2021.
Prudence Crandall Collection. Linda Lear Center for Special Collections and Archives, Connecticut College Library, New London, Connecticut.
"Quindaro." Kansas History Society, kansashistory.gov.
"Quindaro: A Free-State Black Town." Legends of Kansas, legendsofkansas.com.
Schuch, Tom. "The Fayerweathers." New London's Black Heritage Trail, Explore New London, https://visitnewlondon.org/.

Second Congregational Church Records, Norwich. Connecticut State Library digital archives.
Warren, Kim. "Seeking the Promised Land: African American Migrations to Kansas." Civil War on the Western Border, Kansas City Public Library website.
"Western University (Kansas) is Founded." African American Registry website.
Williams, Donald E., Jr. *Prudence Crandall's Legacy: The Fight for Equality in the 1830s, Dred Scott, and Brown v. Board of Education.* Middletown, CT: Wesleyan University Press, 2014.
Woodward, Carl R. "A Profile in Dedication: Sarah Harris and the Fayerweather Family." *New England Galaxy*, Summer 1973.

David Ruggles

"Boycotting Goods Produced by Slaves." Quakers in the World website.
"David Ruggles." Museum of the City of New York, education sheet.
Gerould, Kim. "David Ruggles." University of Massachusetts website.
Goldscheider, Tom. "David Ruggles: Black Abolitionist of the Underground Railroad." Video of live presentation, African Burial Ground National Monument. National Park Service, nps.gov.
Higginbotham, Susan. "From the Underground Railroad to the Water-Cure: David Ruggles," susanhigginbotham.com.
Hodges, Graham. "David Ruggles: The Hazards of Anti-Slavery Journalism." *Freedom Forum* archive, Summer 2000.
———. *David Ruggles: A Radical Black Abolitionist and the Underground Railroad in New York City.* Chapel Hill: University of North Carolina Press, 2010.
———. "David Ruggles Was a Friend to Frederick Douglass, the First Full-Time Black Activist and a Lead Conductor on the Underground Railroad." *Milwaukee Journal Sentinel*, February 14, 2020.
Jaffe, Steven H. "David Ruggles' Committee of Vigilance." *Lapham's Quarterly*, May 21, 2018.
Kolding, Isaac. "The Tedious Heroism of David Ruggles." Commonplace history website, December 2024.
Larson, Julia. "David Ruggles (1810–1849)." City University of New York website.
"New York City Anti-Abolitionist Riots." Wikipedia entry.
"November 20, 1835: New York Committee of Vigilance Founded." Zinn Education Project, zinnedproject.org.
Ruggles, David. "The Abrogation of the Seventh Commandment by the American Churches." Pamphlet, 1835.
———. "The Emancipator, November 2, 1836." Black Abolitionist Archives, University of Detroit Mercy.
———. "Inalienable Rights." *The Liberator*, February 10, 1843.
"A Utopian Community in Florence, Massachusetts." David Ruggles Center for History and Education, Florence, Northampton, Massachusetts.

Pelleman Williams

American Missionary Association Collection. The *Amistad* Research Center, Tilton Memorial Hall, Tulane University, New Orleans, January 2024.

"Arthur Williams, Veteran Teacher, Died in Harness." *New Orleans States*, June 11, 1920.

Carvalho, Joseph, III. "Black Families of Hampden County, Massachusetts: 1650–1865," paper.

Census document, June 1880. New Orleans Parish.

Cockrill, Rachel. "A Timeline of Straight University." Preservation Resource Center of New Orleans, September 29, 2017.

DeVore, Donald E. "Race Relations and Community Development: The Education of Blacks in New Orleans, 1862–1960." Dissertation. Louisiana State University and Agricultural & Mechanical College, 1989.

"Easter Service at St. Philip's P.E. Church." *Weekly Louisianian*, April 8, 1882.

Harris, Mary. Death Certificate. Archives, New Orleans, Louisiana.

Historic New Orleans Archives. 520 Royal Street, New Orleans, January 2024.

Hunter, G. Howard. "Fall of New Orleans and Federal Occupation." 64 Parishes website.

"Men of the Month." *The Crisis*, New Orleans, February 1916.

Musée de FPC, Le. 2336 Esplanade Avenue, New Orleans, January 2024.

Palpini, Kristin, and Chance Viles. "Forgotten: Springfield's Black History Is Nowhere in Sight." *The Valley Advocate*, June 5, 2017.

"Pelleman M. Williams." Blacks @ Dartmouth 1775 to 1960 website.

"Report of the Board of Education for Freedmen." Department of the Gulf, 1864, Daniel Murray Pamphlet Collection, Library of Congress website.

"Straight University." *New Orleans Daily Democrat*, February 26, 1878.

"Straight Up History." Articles on history of Straight University, Preservation Resource Center of New Orleans.

Trotter, James M. "eBook of Music and Some Highly Musical People." Project Gutenberg, February 12, 2009.

"Voices of Progress: 20 Women Who Changed New Orleans." Sylvanie Williams, Historic New Orleans Collection website.

"Williams Death Notice." *Times-Picayune*, New Orleans, September 13, 1882; May 16, 1900; June 12, 1920.

"Williams, Prof. P. M." Resignation Appointment. *New Orleans Republican*, September 3, 1871.

———. Social Notice. *Weekly Louisianian*, September 7, 1871; January 4, 1879.

Maine

Greene, Bob. "Black History in Maine." Video, Thomas Memorial Library website, Cape Elizabeth, Maine, October 14, 2021.

"The History." Malaga Island, Maine State Museum website.

"History of Maine." Maine Statehood, Wikipedia entry.

Kanes, Candace. "Slavery's Defenders and Foes." *Maine History Online*, Maine Historical Society.
"Malaga Island: An Overview of its Cultural and Natural History." Maine Coast Heritage Trust website, July 6, 2009.
Myall, James. "Race and Public Policy in Maine: Past, Present and Future." *Maine Policy Review*, 29, no. 2.
Portland by the Foot Black History Tour. Led by Dugan Murphy, July 19, 2025.
Price, H. H., and Gerald E. Talbot. *Maine's Visible Black History*. Gardiner, ME: Tilbury House, 2006.
"73 Newbury Street: Abyssinian Meeting House." Greater Portland Landmarks website.

Charles Frederick Eastman

"Charles F. Eastman Obituary." *Portland Daily Press*, August 18, 1880, via Newspapers.com.
Community Reports. "The Underground Railroad in Maine: Great Risks, Great Rewards." *Saco Bay News*, August 15, 2023.
Eastman, Charles Frederick, Jr.; Find a Grave website.
Home of Charles Frederick Eastman, Harriet Stephenson Eastman, and her father, Alexander Stephenson. Portland Freedom Trail, The Historical Marker Database website, February 13, 2023.
O'Brien, Andy. "Exploring Black History on Portland's Freedom Trail." Amjambo Africa website, February 28, 2023.
Portland Freedom Trail Pamphlet: Self-Guided Walking Tour. Prepared by Portland Freedom Trail.
Ryden, Tory. "Maine's Pivotal Role in the Underground Railroad." *News Center Maine*, March 1, 2018.
"6 Stops on the Underground Railroad: They Were Part of a Larger Network." New England Historical Society website.
Society Records, 1839–1876. Abyssinian Church in Portland, Maine, Congregational Library and Archives.

Robert Benjamin Lewis

Barnette, Cheryl. "Robert Benjamin Lewis," 2020, https://vocal.media/journal.
Freeman, Mary, Dr. "Abolition and the Underground Railroad in Maine." Video of lecture given on September 7, 2023, Castine Historical Society, via YouTube, https://www.youtube.com/watch?v=fDBadPXYBG8.
Hughes-Warrington, Marnie. "Coloring Universal History: Robert Benjamin Lewis's *Light and Truth* (1843) and William Wells Brown's *The Black Man* (1863)." *Journal of World History*, 20, no. 1 (March 2009), published by University of Hawai'i Press.
Hunt, James. "On the Negro's Place in Nature." *Journal of the Anthropological Society of London*, Vol. 2 (1864), Royal Anthropological Institute of Great Britain and Ireland.
Lewis, Robert B. *Light and Truth*. Google Books. Benjamin F. Roberts, printer, 1844.
"Robert Benjamin Lewis." Maine State Library entry, via their website.

———. Wikipedia entry.
"Robert Benjamin Lewis: Author and Inventor Born." African American Registry website.
"The Southern Argument for Slavery." US History, ushistory.org.

Reuben Ruby

"Celebrating the Diversity and Contributions of Black Communities." Permanent Commission Racial, Indigenous and Tribal Populations, Maine.gov, February 29, 2024.
Goddu, Heather, and Brigitte Reid. "If These Walls Could Talk." *Learn With Moose*, learnwithmoose.maine.gov.
Gray Historical Society Honor Roll.
Greene, Bob. "Reuben Ruby: Hackman, Activist." Maine History Online, project of the Maine Historical Society.
The Liberator, November 1, 1834, p. 1, via newspapers.com.
Middleton, Daniel J. "Reuben Ruby: From Hack Driver to Pioneering Abolitionist." Unique Coloring website.
O'Brien, Andy. "Maine's Abolitionist Movement Launches." Amjambo Africa website, May 7, 2023.
———. "Radical Mainers." *The Bollard*, 2023.
———. "Reuben Ruby and Maine Anti-Slavery Society's Founding." Amjambo Africa website, June 16, 2023.
"Portland Freedom Trail Pamphlet: Self-Guided Walking Tour." Prepared by Portland Freedom Trail.
"Reuben Ruby." Wikipedia entry.
"Reuben Ruby Hack Driver Drives William Lloyd Garrison Around Portland and Facilitates Mtg. With Black Leaders." Niles House—History of the Niles Family and Neighborhood, nilesfamily.me.
"Ruby, Reuben (1798–1878)." Gray, Maine, graymaine.org.

John Brown Russwurm

Burrowes, Carl Patrick; "A Child of the Atlantic: The Maine Years of John Brown Russwurm;" *Maine History*, 47, no. 2 (2013), Digital Commons, University of Maine.
Cairns, Kathleen. "John Russwurm (1799–1851)." *Black Past*, blackpast.org, January 17, 2007.
Curriculum Concepts International. *"Freedom's Journal." Mapping the African American Past*, Columbia University.
Danzy, Nyla. "The Fight against the Erasure of John B. Russwurm." *The Bowdoin Orient*, February 9, 2024.
"Freedom's Journal." Encyclopedia Britannica entry, britannica.com.
———. (New York 1827–1829). Directory of US Newspapers in American Libraries, Library of Congress.
———. Online Archive. Wisconsin Historical Society.

BIBLIOGRAPHY

"Freedom's Journal." 1, no. 2 (March 23, 1827), page 1, via Wisconsin Historical Society website.
James, Winston. *The Struggles of John Brown Russwurm: The Life and Writings of a Pan-Africanist Pioneer, 1799–1851*. New York: New York University Press, 2010. (Access to book description and synopses provided by University of Connecticut Library.)
"John Brown Russwurm." Wikipedia entry.
"John Brown Russwurm Biographical Sketch." Early Alumni of Bowdoin College, George J. Mitchell Department of Special Collections and Archives, Bowdoin Library, online research guides.
"John Brown Russwurm, 1799–1851." Jamaicans Abroad website, 2018.
LeDuff, Kim M. "John Brown Russwurm." Research Starters, ebsco.com.
"Newspapers: *Freedom's Journal*." PBS.org, Black Press.
Phillips, Ohavia. "Honoring the Greats in Journalism and Media: John B. Russwurm." YouTube, https://www.youtube.com/watch?v=B9pa-__UEik, February 13, 2019.
Russwurm, Laurel L. "John Brown Russwurm." russwurm.org.
Russwurm African American Center. John Brown Russwurm Collection, Bowdoin Special Collections, Department of Africana Studies, Bowdoin College.

MASSACHUSETTS
Boston Slavery Exhibit. City of Boston, boston.gov.
Eastman, W. Dean. "1843 Riot on Ann Street, Boston." Primary Research, primaryresearch.org.
"The Legal End of Slavery in Massachusetts." Massachusetts Historical Society, masshist.org.
Massachusetts Court System. "Massachusetts Constitution and the Abolition of Slavery," mass.gov.
Mulligan, Frank. "New Bedford Celebrates Historic Roots with Abolition Row Park, Frederick Douglass Statue." *New Bedford Standard-Times*, posted on New Bedford Historical Society website.
Secondo, Noah. "Abolition and Industrialization, Springfield, Massachusetts, 1830–1870." Harvard University.
"Slavery and Law in 17th Century Massachusetts." Boston National Historical Park, Boston African American National Historic Site. National Park Service, nps.gov.
Stauffer, John. "Boston's Crusade Against Slavery." President and Fellows of Harvard College, 2018.
"A Woman Named Rose." Salem Maritime National Historic Site, National Park Service, nps.gov.

Paul Cuffe
"Cuffe, Paul, Personal and Family Papers." New Bedford Free Public Library, Town of Westport, Massachusetts, website.
"February 10, 1780: Paul Cuffee and Other Free Blacks Petition for the Right to Vote." Zinn Education Project, zinnedproject.org.

Gates, Henry Louis, Jr. "Who Led the First Back-to-Africa Effort?" *The African Americans* television show, PBS website.
"To James Madison from Paul Cuffe, 22 June 1812." Letter, Founders Online, National Archives.
Lamont, Thomas. "Rise to Be a Book." Cuffe Biographer Address, paulcuffe.org.
"Life of Captain Paul Cuffe." Captain Paul Cuffe Center for Inclusion, Massachusetts Maritime Academy.
Mobley, Tianna. "Paul Cuffe & President James Madison: The Transatlantic Emigration Project & the White House." Georgetown Fellow 2020–2022, White House Historical Association website.
"Paul Cuffe." New Bedford Whaling National Historical Park, National Park Service, nps.gov.
"Paul Cuffe: An African American and Native American Heritage Trail." Westport Historical Society, paulcuffe.org, 2022.
"Paul Cuffe: American Ship Owner, Merchant, Pan-Africanist." Encyclopedia Britannica entry, britannica.com.
"Paul Cuffe Biography." Video. *The Daily Bellringer*, January 31, 2021, via YouTube, https://www.youtube.com/watch?v=_KQ_xeVARMU&t=1s.
"Westport Dedication, Monument in Memory of Capt. Paul Cuffee." *New Bedford Evening Standard*, 1913, paulcuffe.org.

Charlotte Forten Grimké

Billington, Ray Allen. *The Journal of Charlotte L. Forten*. Google Books, Northwestern University, 1953.
"Celebrate Black History Month in Salem." Salem: Still Making History, salem.org.
"Charlotte Forten Biography." Video. Salem State University, salemstate.edu.
Exhibit of Charlotte Forten's Biography and Writings. Charlotte Forten Legacy Room, Salem State University.
"Journal of Charlotte L. Forten." Biographical Information and Book Synopsis, The Museum of the American Revolution, March 8, 2023.
"Journal of Charlotte Forten, Free Woman of Color." National Humanities Center, 2007.
Salem Stories Exhibition. Peabody Essex Museum, Salem, Massachusetts.

Prince Hall

Allen, Danielle. "A Forgotten Black Founding Father." *The Atlantic*, March 2021.
"Biography: Prince Hall." Video. Akhase Organization, March 18, 2020.
"Prince Hall." *Africans in America*. WGBH, PBS, pbs.org.
———. The West End Museum, thewestendmuseum.org.
———. Wikipedia entry.
"Prince Hall: Bound for Greatness." Medford Historical Society and Museum, medfordhistorical.org.
"Prince Hall: The Founder of Black Masons in the U.S." Royal, Black & Elite Video Series, July 20, 2023.

Sesay, Chernoh Momodu, Jr. "Freemasons of Color: Prince Hall, Revolutionary Black Boston, and the Origins of Black Freemasonry, 1770–1807." Dissertation, Northwestern University, December 2006.
Tabbert, Mark. "Freemasonry in Colonial America." George Washington's Mount Vernon, mountvernon.org.

Lewis Hayden

"Boston's Own Underground Railroad Conductors: Harriet and Lewis Hayden." City of Boston, boston.gov.
Demortie, Walker. "Lewis Hayden." National Underground Railroad Freedom Center, freedomcenter.org.
"54th Massachusetts Regiment." National Park Service, nps.gov.
"Fighting for Freedom: Lewis Hayden and the Underground Railroad." Video. Boston African American National Historic Site, National Park Service, nps.gov.
"Hayden, Lewis." Notable Kentucky African Americans Database. University of Kentucky Library, University of Kentucky.
Letters to/from Lewis Hayden. Anti-Slavery Collection, Boston Public Library, digitalcommonwealth.org.
"Lewis Hayden." Article on Exhibits, Tufts University website.
———. New Bedford Historical Society, nbhistoricalsociety.org.
———. The West End Museum, Boston, thewestendmuseum.org.
———. Wikipedia entry.
"Lewis Hayden and the Underground Railroad." Massachusetts Secretary of State Pamphlet.
"Lewis and Harriet Hayden." Colored Conventions Project, coloredconventions.org.
"Lewis and Harriet Hayden House." Boston African American National Historic Site, National Park Service, nps.gov.
Musgrave, Tom. "Monument Honors the Work of Lexington Abolitionists Lewis and Harriet Hayden." University of Kentucky, June 18, 2024.
Robboy, Stanley J., and Anita W. Robboy. "Lewis Hayden: From Fugitive Slave to Statesman." *New England Quarterly*, December 1973.

William Cooper Nell

"Abiel Smith School." Boston African American National Historic Site, National Park Service, nps.gov.
"Crisis in Black and White: William Lloyd Garrison, William Cooper Nell, and the Battle Against Slavery, January 1832." Jamaica Plain Historical Society, jphs.org.
"Fighting for Freedom." Article and Video. Revolutionary Spaces, revolutionaryspaces.org.
Nell, William Cooper. "The Colored Patriots of the American Revolution." LibriVox, February 18, 2016.
"William C. Nell," Collections Online, Massachusetts Historical Society.

"William Cooper Nell." Boston National Historical Park, Boston African American National Historic Site, National Park Service, nps.gov.

———. The West End Museum, thewestendmuseum.org.

———. Wikipedia entry.

"William Cooper Nell: Black History Mini Docs." Video. December 17. 2024.

"William Cooper Nell: Smith Court Leader." Boston African American National Historic Site, National Park Service, nps.gov.

Sarah Parker Remond

"African-American Abolitionist Sarah Parker Remond." Royal Holloway University of London, Bedford College.

Coleman, Willi. "Sarah Parker Remond (1824–1894)." Black Past, blackpast.org.

"A Colored Lady Lecturer." Article, Sarah Parker Remond. Google Documents.

"The Negroes in the United States of America: 1862." Address given by Sarah Parker Remond, January 1, 1862, Archives of Women's Political Communication, Iowa State University.

Porter, Dorothy Burnett. "The Remonds of Salem, Massachusetts: A Nineteenth-Century Family Revisited." American Antiquarian Society.

Robinson, Sarah. "Sarah Parker Remond: A Trailblazing African American Female Abolitionist in Manchester." *Global Threads*, The Centers for the Studies of British Slavery, Science and Industry Museum.

"Sarah Parker Remond." Case Study, *Women's Suffrage*, suffrageresources.org.uk.

———. Collections Online, Massachusetts Historical Society.

———. Wikipedia entry.

"Sarah Parker Remond Naturalization Papers." The National Archives, United Kingdom, nationalarchives.gov.uk.

New Hampshire

Cox, Stephen Lawrence. "Power, Oppression and Liberation: New Hampshire Abolitionism and the Radical Critique of Slavery, 1825–1850." University of New Hampshire doctoral dissertation, Fall 1980.

Cunningham, Valerie. "A Brief History of Enslaved, Portsmouth, N.H." Posted on Seacoast New Hampshire website, 1999.

Dixon, David T. "A Black New Hampshire Family Fights for Freedom." Emerging Civil War website, April 2, 2022.

Eaton, Aurore. "Looking Back: A Last Look at New Hampshire's Anti-Slavery Movement: A Convention, a Party, and a Parade . . ." *New Hampshire Union Leader*, September 22, 2024.

Exeter Historical Society. "Strong and Brave Fellows: New Hampshire's Black Revolutionary War Soldiers and Sailors, 1775–1784." Video of live presentation, Exeter TV, October 7, 2020.

Harper, Douglas. "Slavery in New Hampshire." *Slavery in the North*, slavenorth.com, 2003.

Little, Becky. "Slavery Persisted in New England Until the 19th Century." History.com, July 12, 2023.
"Portsmouth Black Heritage Trail." Black Heritage Trail of New Hampshire, 2018.
Robinson, J. Dennis. "Whittier's Anti-Slavery Ode to N.H." Posted on Seacoast New Hampshire website, 1998.
Whipple, Prince. "1779 Petition to the New Hampshire Government for the Abolition of Slavery." National Park Service, nps.gov.

Julia Williams Garnet

"A Few Black Students with Books in Their Hands Set the Granite State on Fire." NHTI, Concord's Community College, March 9, 2022.
"August 10, 1835: Destruction of Noyes Academy," Zinn Education Project, zinnedproject.org.
"Julia Williams." Rootsweb website.
———. Wikipedia entry.
"Julia Williams Garnet." Boston National Historical Park, Boston African American National Historic Site, National Park Service, nps.gov.
"Noyes Academy." Town of Canaan, New Hampshire. website.
Pinheiro, Holly A., Jr. "Julia W. Garnet's Civil War Activism." *Black Perspectives*, December 14, 2022.
WMUR-TV. "Teacher Preserves Story of Noyes Academy, Its Students." Video. February 26, 2021.

Ona Marie Judge

Chervinsky, Lindsay M. "The Remarkable Story of Ona Judge." White House Historical Association website, October 21, 2019.
Dunbar, Erica Armstrong. "Never Caught: The Washingtons' Relentless Pursuit of Their Runaway Slave Ona Judge." Atria, 2017.
"Ona Judge." Wikipedia entry.
"Ona Judge: A Woman Who Escaped Slavery and the Washingtons." Video. George Washington's Mount Vernon, mountvernon.org, February 27, 2019.
"Ona Judge Escapes to Freedom." Independence National Historical Park, National Park Service, nps.gov.
"Ona Marie Judge Staines." New Hampshire Radical History website, June 2, 2021.
Quintin, Kira. "'I am free now': Ona Judge's Escape from Slavery and George Washington's Hunt to Get Her Back." Boundary Stones website, WETA Virginia, May 21, 2024.

Prince Whipple

Cunningham, Valerie. "Prince Whipple (1750–1796)." Black Past, blackpast.org, July 13, 2007.
Davidson, Rick. "Gravesites of William Whipple and His Slave Prince Whipple." Video. June 7, 2024.

"Moffatt-Ladd House Was Also Home to Prince Whipple." Video. WMUR-TV, February 8, 2024.
Portsmouth Athenaeum. "Prince Whipple Records."

Harriet Wilson
Fernald, Jodie R. "Slavery in New Hampshire: Profitable Godliness to Racial Consciousness." University of New Hampshire master's thesis, Winter 2007.
Gardner, Eric. "This Attempt of Their Sister: Harriet Wilson's 'Our Nig' From Printer to Readers." *New England Quarterly*, June 1993.
"Harriet Wilson, Author Born." African American Registry website.
Harriet Wilson Project. "Milford, Harriet Wilson and the Anti-Slavery Movement." Black heritage tour pamphlet, 2005.
Our Nig. Digital book. Standard ebooks website.
Rodolico, Jack. "Early Novel Written by Free Black Woman Called Out Racism Among Abolitionists." *Weekend Edition*, NPR, February 15, 2020.
Sylvia, Andrew. "Tour Provides Look at African-American History in Milford." *The Union Leader*, October 26, 2019.

NEW YORK
Abolishing Slavery: The Battle over Abolition, 1830–1865. Exhibit Introduction, Museum of the City of New York.
"Abolition." Freethought Trail. Council for Secular Humanism, 2025.
"Abolitionism." New York Heritage Digital Collections: A Project of the Empire State Library Network.
Brathwaite, Jamila Shabazz. "The Black Vigilance Movement in Nineteenth-Century New York City." City University of New York Academic Works, 2014.
Diouf, Sylviane A. "New York City's Slave Market." New York Public Library, nypl.org, June 29, 2015.
"History of Slavery in New York." New York Historical Society, slaveryinnewyork.org.
"History of Slavery in New York (State)." Wikipedia entry.
Mosterman, Andrea C. *The Forgotten History of Slavery in New York*. Ithaca, NY: Cornell University Press, 2025.
"New York: Douglass Family South Street Home Site." National Park Service, nps.gov, April 24, 2023.
"New York Draft Riots." History.com.
"New York Manumission Society." Encyclopedia Britannica entry, britannica.com.
"New York Slave Rebellion of 1712." Encyclopedia Britannica entry, britannica.com.
Race and Antebellum New York City. "The New York Manumission Society." Examination Days, The New York African Free School Collection, New York Historical Society.
———. "Slavery in New York." Examination Days, The New York African Free School Collection, New York Historical Society.

Thomas, Holly Werner. "Slavery in New York." *CRM: The Journal of Heritage Stewardship* 3, no. 2 (Summer 2006), New York Historical Society, via National Park Service, nps.gov.

Wilson, Sherrill D. "Blacks." The Encyclopedia of New York City.

Henry Highland Garnet

"December 23, 1815: Henry Highland Garnet Born." Zinn Education Project, zinnedproject.org.

"Five Minute Histories: Henry Highland Garnet Park." Baltimore Heritage Video Presentation, YouTube. youtube.com/watch?v=SCBbZmDOrfQ, July 19, 2023.

"From Abolitionist to Diplomat: Henry Highland Garnet and Early Relations with Liberia." National Museum of American Diplomacy, February 21, 2024.

Garnet, Henry Highland. "A Memorial Discourse, February 12, 1865." Joseph M. Wilson, Philadelphia, 1865, via Google Books.

"Garnet's Call to Rebellion." Africans in America project, PBS.org.

Genz, Michelle. "Solomon's Wisdom." Special to the *Washington Post*, March 7, 1999, p. F01, via innercity.org.

"Henry Highland Garnet." Africans in America, PBS.org.

———. Biography.com, A&E, April 2, 2014.

———. Examination Days, The New York African Free School Collection, New York Historical Society.

———. Wikipedia entry.

Ortiz, Paul. "One of History's Foremost Anti-Slavery Organizers Is Often Left Out of the Black History Month Story." *Time* magazine, time.com, January 31, 2018.

"Reverend Henry Highland Garnet: An Important Figure in the Abolitionist Movement." Hart Cluett Museum, Troy, New York.

Shernbondy, Jeanette E. "'Let the Monster Perish!' Rev. Henry Highland Garnet's 1865 Address in the Congressional Chapel." Common Sense Eastern Shore, May 23, 2023.

Elizabeth Jennings Graham

"Black History Stories Most People Don't Know." GooseGooseDuck, YouTube, https://www.youtube.com/shorts/E04xAd1Ytz8, December 30, 2024.

"Elizabeth Jennings." Early African New York, Columbia University, teachingforchange.org.

"Elizabeth Jennings Graham." Fact Sheet, Activist New York Series, Museum of the City of New York.

"Her name was Elizabeth Jennings Graham. Do You Know Her Story?" New York Transit Museum website.

Hewitt, John H. "The Search for Elizabeth Jennings, Heroine of a Sunday Afternoon in New York City." *New York History* 71, no. 4 (October 1990), Fenimore Art Museum, p. 386.

"I Did Not Get Off the Car." Miller Center website, University of Virginia.

"July 16, 1854: Elizabeth Jennings Graham." Zinn Education Project, zinnedproject.org.
Lewis, David. "Elizabeth Jennings Graham." Black Past, blackpast.org, November 4, 2013.
Lewis, Sylvia Wong. "Elizabeth Jennings." Narrative Network website, March 2, 2013.
New York Daily Tribune. Chronicling America, July 19, 1854, via Library of Congress website, Digital Newspapers.

Solomon Northup

Anderson, Sonja. "Solomon Northup's 'Twelve Years a Slave' Came to an End as He Regained His Long-Awaited Freedom on This Day in 1853." *Smithsonian* magazine, January 4, 2025.
Fiske, David. "Twelve Years a Slave: Solomon Northup of Minerva." Adirondack Almanack Community Bulletin Board, August 8, 2013.
Fiske, David, Clifford W. Brown, and Rachel Seligman. *Solomon Northrup: The Complete Story of the Author of "Twelve Years a Slave."* Bloomsbury Publishing, 2013, via Google Books.
Jones, William D. "Solomon Northup." 64parishes.org, October 4, 2024.
Liberatore, Wendy. "Despite Film, Book, Research, Solomon Northup Mysteries Remain." *Times Union*, November 25, 2023.
Martinez, Melinda. "Alexandria Museum Hosts Solomon Northup Traveling Exhibit." *Town Talk*, March 24, 2025.
Northup, Solomon. *Twelve Years a Slave*. Buffalo, NY: Derby & Miller, 1853. Digital version via University of North Carolina, Documenting the American South Project.
Rothman, Adam. "The Horrors '12 Years a Slave' Couldn't Tell." Al Jazeera America, January 18, 2014.
"Solomon Northup." Encyclopedia Britannica entry, britannica.com.
"Solomon Northup Before and After Enslavement / From Slavery to Freedom in New York State." PBS Learning Media for Teachers, Connecticut Public Television.
"Solomon Northup Describes a Slave Market, 1841." The American Yawp Reader, Stanford University Press.
"Solomon Northup: 12 Years a Slave." Documentary. C-SPAN, September 25, 2017.
Tsapina, Olga. "Where Solomon Northup Was a Slave." *The Huntington*, March 4, 2014.
Willard, Lucas. "Retracing the Steps of Solomon Northup in Saratoga Springs." WMAC, Northeast Public Radio, February 27, 2014.

James McCune Smith

Douglass, Frederick. *My Bondage and My Freedom*. 1855. Internet Archive via University of Pittsburgh Library System.
"Draft Riot of 1863." Encyclopedia Britannica entry, britannica.com.
"From the Stage: James McCune Smith." Colored Conventions Project, coloredconventions.org.

Greene, Bryan. "America's First Black Physician Sought to Heal a Nation's Persistent Illness;" *Smithsonian* magazine, February 26, 2021.
"James McCune Smith." CHAAMP Resources, Resources on History of African Americans in the Medical Professions, University of Virginia.
———. Wikipedia entry.
"James McCune Smith Pharmacy." Mapping the African American Past. JP Morgan Chase Foundation, Columbia Center for New Media Teaching and Learning.
Murphy, Matthew. "'They Deliberately Set Fire to It . . . Simply Because It Was the Home of Unoffending Colored Orphan Children': The New York Draft Riots and the Burning of the Colored Orphan Asylum." *New York Historical*, nyhistory.org, July 16, 2013.
"Rediscovering the Life and Legacy of James McCune Smith." Video. *New York Historical*, nyhistory.org.
Smith, James McCune. "A Lecture on the Haytien Revolutions." Transcript. New York: Daniel Fanshaw, 1841.
Stauffer, John, ed. *The Works of James McCune Smith*. Oxford, UK: Oxford University Press, 2006, via Google Books.

RHODE ISLAND

"Black Rhode Islanders." Rhode Island Department of State website, 2025.
"Bowen's Wharf." Rhode Island Slave History Medallions, rishm.org.
Chace, Elizabeth Buffum. *Anti-Slavery Reminiscences*. Central Falls, RI: E. L. Freeman and Sons, 1891, via Ohio History Connection, Wilbur H. Siebert Underground Railroad Collection, ohiomemory.org.
DeSimone, Russell. "Narrative of an Ashaway Teenager's Role in the Underground Railroad Rediscovered." Small State, Big History website, February 23, 2019.
Lemons, J. Stanley. "Rhode Island and the Slave Trade." *Rhode Island History* 60, no. 4, Rhode Island Historical Society, p. 95.
Little, Becky. "Slavery Persisted in New England Until the 19th Century." History.com, June 29, 2020, updated May 27, 2025.
"March 1, 1784: Rhode Island Passes Gradual Emancipation Act." Zinn Education Project, zinnedproject.org.
McBurney, Christian. "An Enslaved Mother Rescues Her Family from Being Transported to the South—and Spurs a Law Change." Small State, Big History website, January 22. 2022.
"Newport Establishes Port Marker Project." Newport Middle Passage website.
"Slavery, the Slave Trade, and Brown University." *Slavery and Justice Report* (digital edition), Brown University Steering Committee.
Zilian, Fred. "Rhode Island Dominates North American Slave Trade in the 18th Century." Small State, Big History website, June 28, 2020.

George T. Downing

Chaput, Erik, and Russell J. DeSimone. "George T. Downing and the Black Convention Movement." Small State, Big History website, September 16, 2023.

Gardner-Davis, Tyran. "The Fight for Black Mobility: Traveling to Mid-Century Conventions—George T. Downing." Colored Conventions Project, coloredconventions.org, Spring 2013.

"George T. Downing." Fair Street Newport blog, August 11, 2009.

———. Rhode Island Heritage Hall of Fame, riheritagehalloffame.com.

———. Wikipedia entry.

"George T. Downing and Family." Image and description, Collections Online, Massachusetts Historical Society.

McBride, Colin. "George T. Downing (1819–1903)." Black Past, blackpast.org, October 23, 2017.

"Remembering Our Founders: George T. Downing." Improved Order of Patriotic Odd Fellows, guoof.org.

Theresags. "George T. Downing." Gilded Age in Color website, February 10, 2015.

Wijaya, May. "The World Was His Oyster: George T. Downing." rhodetour.org.

George Fayerweather III

Clark, Emily. "Sarah Harris Fayerweather." Project of Connecticut Humanities, Connecticuthistory.org, June 10, 2024.

Cotter, Betty J. "Fayerweathers Gather to Honor Ancestors." *The Independent*, August 23, 2012.

Duncan, David. "Blacksmiths in the 1800s." The Blacksmiths Company website.

"Fayerweather House." www.fayerweatherhouse.8m.net/.

Fayerweather Papers. University Archives and Special Collections, University of Rhode Island.

"George Fayerweather." Wikipedia entry.

"George Fayerweather III." Find a Grave entry, Old Fernwood Cemetery, South Kingstown, Rhode Island.

"'No Taxation without Representation': Black Voting in Connecticut." Project of Connecticut Humanities, Connecticuthistory.org, August 16, 2021.

Normen, Elizabeth J., ed. *African American Connecticut Explored*. Middletown, CT: Wesleyan University Press / Garnet Books, 2016.

Schuch, Tom. "The Fayerweathers." New London's Black Heritage Trail, visitnewlondon.org.

Isaac Rice

"Abolition and Anti-Abolition in Newport, 1835–1866." Newport Historical Society. newporthistory.org, June 8, 2020.

Dumpson, Kimberly. "'My Beloved, O My Beloved': Celebrating Love and the Epistolary Tradition This Valentine's Day." Rhode Island College, our.ric.edu, February 14, 2022.

"Honoring Black History: The Underground Railroad in Rhode Island." Channel 12, WPRI.com, February 25, 2022.
"Isaac Rice." Rhode Island African American Data. Rhode Island Genealogy Trails website, from *Negroes of Rhode Island*, by Charles A. Battle, 1932.
"References to Named Enslaved/Free Persons of Color in Dark Work: The Business of Slavery in Rhode Island." Rhode Island Historical Society, rihs.org.
Rice, John M. "Frederick Douglass and His Abolitionist Friends in Newport and New Bedford." *Newport History*, newporthistory.org.

VERMONT

"Alexander Twilight." Wikipedia entry.
Brown, Lydia, Elodie Reed, and Mitch Wertlieb. "The History of Slavery in Vermont, Across New England." Vermont Public, February 20, 2020.
"Building Communities: Abolition," *Freedom and Unity*, Vermont Historical Society, 2006, updated 2021.
Guyette, Elise A. *Discovering Black Vermont: African American Farmers in Hinesburgh, 1790–1890*. Burlington: University of Vermont Press, 2010.
"July 2, 1777: Vermont Officially Abolished Slavery." Zinn Education Project, zinnproject.org.
"New Frontier: The Fourteenth State." *Freedom and Unity*, Vermont Historical Society, 2006, updated 2021.
"Vermont African American Heritage Trail Brochure." Champlain Valley National Heritage Partnership, vermontvacation.com.
"Vermont 1777: Early Steps Against Slavery." National Museum of African American History and Culture, nmaahc.si.edu.
Williamson, Jane. Interview, October 31, 2024.

Jeffrey Brace

"The Heroic Jeffrey Brace." The American Revolution Institute, americanrevolutioninstitute.org, September 25, 2020.
"Jeffrey Brace: First African American Citizen of Poultney." 200 Years of History in Vermont, Poultney Historical Society.
"Jeffrey Brace: What Does Jeffrey Brace's Story Tell Us about the Challenges Faced by Early Black Vermonters?" *Vermont History Explorer*, vermonthistoryexplorer.org.
Keck, Nina. "Vermont Town Honors Former Slave's Life with Historical Marker." Voice of America, voanews.com, November 1, 2009.
"The Story of Jeffrey Brace." Video of live presentation, Northwest Access Television, February 21, 2018.
"This Place in History: Jeffrey Brace." Video. Vermont Historical Society, May 21, 2022.
Winter, Kari J. "The Strange Career of Benjamin Franklin Prentiss, Antislavery Lawyer." *Vermont History* (Summer/Fall 2011).
———. "The Blind African Slave." Video of live presentation, Museum of the American Revolution, March 2, 2022.

———, organizer. "Labor's Fruit: The Story of Jeffrey Brace." Just Buffalo Literary Center, June 17, 2023.

Andrew Harris

"Andrew Harris: Vermont's Forgotten Abolitionist." Video. *This Place in History*, Vermont Historical Society website, January 19, 2017.

Harris, Andrew. "May 15, 1839: The Emancipator." Address to American Anti-Slavery Society, Black Abolitionist Archives.

"Liberty Party." Encyclopedia Britannica entry, britannica.com.

Morrison, R. J. "The Real Story of Andrew Harris." *The Vermont Cynic*, February 6, 2022.

Thornton, Kevin Pierce. "Andrew Harris: Vermont's Forgotten Abolitionist." *Vermont History* (Summer/Fall 2015), Vermont Historical Society.

———. "Postscript: Andrew Harris at the University of Vermont." *Vermont History* (Winter/Spring 2018), Vermont Historical Society.

Lemuel Haynes

"Battle of Lexington." Lemuel Haynes, Video of Recitation Reenactment. National Park Service, nps.gov, April 14, 2021.

Bushnell, Mark. "Then Again: A Black Preacher's Rise to Prominence,. *VTDigger*, April 21, 2019.

Dixon, Euell A. "Lemuel Haynes." Black Past, blackpast.org, January 18, 2007.

Gerrish, Alex. "Lemuel Haynes: America's First Black Ordained Minister." ConnecticutHistory.org, April 17, 2023.

Haynes, Lemuel. "Liberty Further Extended: Or Free Thoughts on the Illegality of Slave-Keeping, 1776." Teaching American History, teachingamericanhistory.org.

———. "The Nature and Importance of True Republicanism with a Few Suggestions Favorable to Independence." Delivered at Rutland, Vermont, July 4, 1801. digitalcommons@university of Nebraska, Lincoln.

"Lemuel Haynes." *Africans in America*, WGBH, pbs.org.

———. Video. *This Place in History*, Vermont Historical Society website, October 3, 2019.

———. Wikipedia entry.

Louden Langley

Bowman, Sarah. "Louden Langley: A Soldier Without Limitations." *The Island Packet*, May 21, 2015.

"Descendant of Early Black Vermonter Talks about His Family History." *VTDigger*, November 22, 2020.

"54th Massachusetts Regiment." National Park Service, nps.gov.

Fuller, James, ed. "The Letters of Louden S. Langley." *Vermont History* (Summer/Fall 1999), Vermont Historical Society.

BIBLIOGRAPHY

Guyette, Elise A. *Discovering Black Vermont: African American Farmers in Hinesburgh, 1790–1890*. Burlington: University of Vermont Press, 2010.
Kelley, Kevin J. "Hinesburg's Black History." *Seven Days*, June 3, 2010.
"The Legacy of the 1st South Carolina Volunteers." National Park Service, nps.gov.
"Louden Langley." National Park Service, nps.gov.
"Louden Langley's Fight for Freedom." Video. *The Island Packet*, May 23, 2015.
Williamson, Jane, ed. "'I don't get fair play here': A Black Vermonter Writes Home." *Vermont History* (Winter/Spring 2007), Vermont Historical Society.

About the Author

Gail Braccidiferro MacDonald is a retired professor of journalism following a long career at the University of Connecticut. A veteran journalist and lifelong lover of history, she has authored several local history books and frequently gives historic-themed tours and talks. She lives in southeastern Connecticut with her beloved pets.

www.ingramcontent.com/pod-product-compliance
Ingram Content Group UK Ltd.
Pitfield, Milton Keynes, MK11 3LW, UK
UKHW042026140426
5221IPUK00002B/30